Case Studies in
Educational Psychology

Case Studies in Educational Psychology

Elementary School Grades

Patricia P. Willems
and
Alyssa R. Gonzalez-DeHass

ROWMAN & LITTLEFIELD
Lanham • Boulder • New York • London

Published by Rowman & Littlefield
A wholly owned subsidiary of The Rowman & Littlefield Publishing Group, Inc.
4501 Forbes Boulevard, Suite 200, Lanham, Maryland 20706
www.rowman.com

Unit A, Whitacre Mews, 26–34 Stannary Street, London SE11 4AB

British Library Cataloguing in Publication Information Available

Library of Congress Cataloging-in-Publication Data
Names: Willems, Patricia P., 1972– author. | Gonzalez-DeHass, Alyssa R., author.
Title: Case studies in educational psychology : elementary school grades / Patricia P. Willems and Alyssa R. Gonzalez-DeHass.
Description: Lanham : Rowman & Littlefield, [2017] | Includes bibliographical references and index.
Identifiers: LCCN 2017039932 (print) | LCCN 2017042459 (ebook) | ISBN 9781475839166 (Electronic) | ISBN 9781475839142 (cloth : alk. paper) | ISBN 9781475839159 (pbk. : alk. paper)
Subjects: LCSH: Educational psychology–United States–Case studies. | Middle school education–United States. | Middle school education–Social aspects–United States.
Classification: LCC LB1051 (ebook) | LCC LB1051 .W58895 2017 (print) | DDC 370.15–dc23
LC record available at https://lccn.loc.gov/2017039932

♾™ The paper used in this publication meets the minimum requirements of American National Standard for Information Sciences—Permanence of Paper for Printed Library Materials, ANSI/NISO Z39.48–1992.

Printed in the United States of America

Dear Logan, Emma, Gavin, Ava, and Maddox:
May your classrooms be places of discovery, exploration, and inspiration. May your teachers ignite your imagination and instill a love of learning, so that you are able to appreciate your unique potential and reach for the stars.

Dear Future Teachers:
It takes heart and patience to shape little minds. You are the true superheroes.

Contents

Introduction

Why Case Instruction?

Case studies present real-life classroom scenarios that reflect the challenges actual classroom teachers experience in today's classrooms. They provide a vehicle to prepare preservice teachers for future classroom decision making. Utilizing case studies is particularly vital for educational psychology courses that do not require a field component where students would have a chance to apply information firsthand in the schools. Case study learning experiences are the next best thing to actual classroom opportunities, and they may even be an important first step. They provide students the chance to see the relevance of educational psychology material and afford them an opportunity to practice hypothetical teacher decision making.

The cases in this text depict key challenges that elementary school teachers face in today's schools: kindergarten readiness, teasing, bullying, academic honesty and plagiarism, making time for recess, disruptive and defiant behavior, the use of rewards and punishments, teaching respect, gender stereotypes, the effects of social media, the use of technology in the classroom, diverse learners, bridging home and school cultures, helicopter parenting, parent involvement, and juggling instructional time amid high-stakes testing. However, these classroom dilemmas are embedded within the domains of learning common across coursework in educational psychology: human development, individual differences, learning theories, motivation, classroom management, instruction, and assessment practices.

Engaging in discussion and decision making about critical classroom challenges may have enormous benefits for preservice teachers' learning, and these include gaining an appreciation for the realities of classroom teaching, opportunities for authentic learning experiences, scaffolding of critical thinking skills, and becoming engaged and motivated in learning about educational psychology (Gonzalez-DeHass & Willems, 2015). Because of their narrative nature, cases engage students' interest and capture their attention (Ching, 2011). Further, case instruction may assist preservice teachers in bridging theory and practice (Engle & Faux, 2006; Patrick, Anderman, Bruening, & Duffin, 2011), promote students' capacity to apply psychological constructs and their critical analysis of educational situations (Bruning et al., 2008; PytlikZillig et al., 2011), and encourage students' intrinsic motivation for learning (DeMarco, Hayward, & Lynch, 2002; Mayo, 2002).

TO GET THE MOST OUT OF CASE INSTRUCTION

This case study book presents coverage of all the main topical areas in educational psychology and provides open-ended questions targeting the specific theories. Instructors can use these questions as discussion or incorporate them into assignments. Identified key practices in case study instruction may be particularly helpful for students' learning: establishing a collaborative community of learners; encouraging perspective taking of various stakeholders in a case; scaffolding students' reflection and critical thinking skills during case analyses; revisiting cases using different theoretical viewpoints, or at different points in the course; and transitioning class discussions into a culminating writing assignment (Gonzalez-DeHass & Willems, 2015).

The cases in this text have been developed with these tips in mind. Case study instruction should encourage students to consider classroom solutions from the viewpoint of different classroom stakeholders (Heitzmann, 2008; Sudzina, 1997). Some of the cases are written from the student's perspective, while others may be from the teacher's standpoint, and we encourage you to examine the challenges in the case from multiple stakeholders' viewpoints. For example, case 16, "Managing Defiant Students," allows the reader to consider the viewpoint of the teacher, student, parents, and the assistant principal in regards to a classroom with defiant behavior and classroom management concerns. Another suggestion for effective case instruction involves instructor and students revisiting cases at a later point in their course. During initial discussions, students become versed in the language of individual theories and their application to authentic classroom challenges, but as they gain more experience with case analysis they become more reflective, more cognizant of effective practices, and less likely to resort to the simplest answer (Sudzina, 1997). For example, case 4, "Cheating in the Technology Age," can be first introduced in the development lesson to discuss the impact of social media on young students' development of morality. However, the instructor could return to the case later in the course when covering topics on classroom management and discuss consequences that could be appropriately applied for this age group. In addition, this case study could be revisited from the angle of parent involvement where students could brainstorm ideas of how to involve parents in the discussion of plagiarism and the internet with students of this age.

Sometimes this discussion will take place within small-group work as students brainstorm solutions to teaching challenges before joining in whole-class discussion. Regardless of group format, when students are encouraged to talk about classroom teaching practices it cultivates a collaborative learning environment that engages them in decision making under the guidance of their course instructor.

STANDARDS AND PRINCIPLES

The cases featured in this book can be linked to the *Learner-Centered Psychological Principles* published by the American Psychological Association (APA) (Learner-Centered Principles Work Group of the American Psychological Association's Board of Educational Affairs, 1997) and the model core teaching standards of the Interstate Teacher Assessment and Support Consortium (INTASC) (Council of Chief State School Officers, 2011). We chose to include these principles and standards due to their relevance to the field of educational psychology and their commitment to improving education. The APA learner-centered psychological principles offer a useful structure for improving schools by integrating improved teaching practices centered on the learner and aimed at the active learning process. There are fourteen APA learner-centered psychological principles under four factors: cognitive and metacognitive factors, motivational and affective factors, developmental and social factors, and individual differences factors. Each factor includes a set of principles that relate to that factor, as well as an in-depth description of each principle (the full document may be viewed at https://www.apa.org/ed/governance/bea/learner-centered.pdf).

The INTASC Model Core Teaching Standards describe essential effective teaching ideologies for the sole purpose of improving student success. These standards are applicable across all grades and school subjects and are relevant to the field of educational psychology. There are ten INTASC Model Core Teaching Standards that are divided into four categories: the learner and learning, content knowledge, instructional practice, and professional responsibility. In general, the INTASC Model Core Teaching Standards emphasize the importance of student-centered instructional methods that appreciate individual differences between learners and where students apply the knowledge they learn to the real world (the full document can be viewed at www.ccsso.org/documents/2011/intasc_model_core_teaching_standards_2011.pdf).

Standards and Principles: Linking to the Cases

The themes outlined in both the INTASC Model Core Teaching Standards and the APA learner-centered psychological principles provide a framework for which to apply the educational psychology theories the case studies in this book are centered on. The link between the standards and principles and the theories found in the cases allows students and instructors to make connections between standards in the field for effective teaching practices and theoretical knowledge. For example, the second factor in the APA learner-centered psychological principles is motivational and affective factors which house motivational and emotional influences on learning and intrinsic motivation to learn. These two learner-centered psychological principles tie to part IV of the case book which is the motivation section and contains cases 13–14 that introduce various aspects of motivation such as extrinsic and intrinsic motivation, self-efficacy, self-regulation, and Maslow's hierarchy of needs.

Similarly, the educational psychology concepts and theories addressed in the cases are able to be associated with the INTASC Model Core Teaching Standards. For instance, the first category of the INTASC Model Core Teaching Standards is the learner and learning, and it contains three standards: learner development, learning differences, and learning environments. This category's first standard on learner development ties to the development section of the case book comprised of cases 1–4. The first four cases of the book all deal with numerous aspects of human development, and the cases suggested theories include various developmental concepts such as cognitive, social, psychosocial, and moral development. The second standard under this category is learning differences, and it can be directly linked to part II of the case book, the individual differences and diversity section, which is comprised of cases 5–8. These case studies' topics range from a variety of aspects of learner differences including gender, intelligence, and cultural diversity. Finally, the third standard in this category is learning environments which relate to part III of the case book, "Learning Theories," composed of cases 9–12. These cases have themes that cover various aspects relating directly to creating a productive student learning environment such as the use of operant conditioning and reducing negative responses, applications of cognitive theories and information processing, learner styles, and applications of social cognitive theory.

In addition, a second book, *Problem Solving for Challenges in Today's Secondary Schools: Cases in Educational Psychology*, presents cases that depict significant challenges that teachers face in today's middle and high schools: academic honesty and internet plagiarism, complaining and arguing about grades, backtalk and disrespect, cyberbullying, adolescent cliques, academic pressures of high school, encouraging female students in STEM learning, the power of social media, cell phones in the classroom, encounters with difficult parents, and finding and grading meaningful alternative assessment options.

REFERENCES

Bruning, R., Siwatu, K. O., Liu, X., PytlikZillig, L. M., Horn, C., Sic, S., & Carslon, D. (2008). Introducing teaching cases with face-to-face and computer-mediated discussion: Two multi-classroom quasi-experiments. *Contemporary Educational Psychology, 33*, 299–326.

Ching, C. P. (2011). Preservice teachers' use of educational theories in classroom and behavior management course: A case based approach. *Procedia: Social and Behavioral Sciences, 29*, 1209–1217.

Council of Chief State School Officers. (2011, April). Interstate teacher assessment and support consortium (InTASC) model core teaching standards: A resource for state dialogue. Washington, DC: CC550. Retrieved February 20, 2017, from www.ccsso.org/documents/2011/intasc_model _core_teaching_ standards_2011.pdf.

DeMarco, R., Hayward, L., & Lynch, M. (2002). Nursing students' experiences with strategic approaches to case-based instruction: A replication and comparison study between two disciplines. *Journal of Nursing Education, 41*(4), 165–174.

Engle, R. A. & Faux, R. B. (2006). Towards productive disciplinary engagement of prospective teachers in educational psychology: Comparing two methods of case-based instruction. *Teaching Educational Psychology, 1*(2), 1–22.

Gonzalez-DeHass, A. R. & Willems, P. P. (2015). Case study instruction in educational psychology: Implications for teacher preparation. In M. Li & Y. Zhao (Eds.), *Exploring Learning and Teaching in Higher Education.* Springer.

Heitzmann, R. (2008). Case study instruction in teacher education: Opportunity to develop students' critical thinking, school smarts and decision making. *Education, 128*(4), 523–543.

Learner-Centered Principles Work Group of the American Psychological Association's Board of Educational Affairs (1997, November). Learner-centered psychological principles: A framework for school redesign. Retrieved February 20, 2017, from https://www.apa.org/ed/governance/bea/learner-centered.pdf.

Mayo, J. A. (2002). Case-based instruction: A technique for increasing conceptual application in introductory psychology. *Journal of Constructivist Psychology, 15*, 65–74.

Patrick, H., Anderman, L. H., Bruening, P. S., & Duffin, L. C. (2011). The role of educational psychology in teacher education: Three challenges for educational psychologists. *Educational Psychologist, 46*(2), 71–83.

PytlikZillig, L. M., Horn, C. A., Bruning, R., Bell, S., Liu, X., Siwatu, K. O., Bodvarsson, M. C., Doyoung, K., & Carlson, D. (2011). Face-to-face versus computer-mediated discussion of teaching cases: Impacts on preservice teachers' engagement, critical analyses, and self-efficacy. *Contemporary Educational Psychology, 36*, 302–312.

Sudzina, M. R. (1997). Case study as a constructivist pedagogy for teaching educational psychology. *Educational Psychology Review, 9*(2), 199–218.

Part I

HUMAN DEVELOPMENT

Kindergarten Readiness

Suggested Theories: Cognitive Development, Psychosocial and Socioemotional Development, and Classroom Management
Teacher Challenges: School readiness, Scaffolding Learning, and Classroom Misbehavior
Student Level: Kindergarten

As her kindergarten students return from recess, Mrs. Arnett overhears a conversation some of the students are having. "Myron did not cheat, cheating is when you take pieces off the board and hide them and then use them later!" says Margo. "Yeah, but he ran around the monkey bars and not under them like we were supposed to, and that is cheating!" says Russell. "No, because he did not take anything!" replies Margo. The students then all agree with Margo and continue to play. The students resolve this problem themselves and eventually find their way to their seats in the classroom.

As the students settle back into the classroom, it is time for their morning snack and a chance to refuel before turning to the day's next learning activity. Today the students are watching an educational video while they eat a light snack of graham crackers. Suddenly Luke stands up and exclaims irritably, "Hey! Russell got more than me!" Mrs. Arnett calmly replies, "Luke, Russell has two crackers because his are very small. When you place his two crackers side by side they are the same size as the one you got."

Luke seems puzzled; however, before he has a chance to respond, other students begin to complain about Russell getting two crackers as well. Mrs. Arnett decides to go around the room and break all of the large graham crackers into two pieces. Suddenly all of the students are happy and quickly go back to watching the video. Mrs. Arnett smiles; after all, it is just another typical day in her kindergarten class.

However, as the video ends and the teacher directs students to finish their drawings from the morning's reading at story time, she steps into another altercation occurring with Luke. Luke stops her on her way to the desk to tattle on Margo. "I was using the green pencil first—make her give it back, it's mine!" Luke yells. He and Margo, who are part of one group, are quarrelling over the bin filled with colored pencils that is in the center of their table. "No, it is mine now, use something else!" Margo shouts back.

Mrs. Arnett interrupts Luke's reply and makes her way back to their table while saying, "OK let's not argue, we all need to share the pencils. Now Margo give Luke back the color he was using and then you may use it when he is finished." Margo replies in a whiny tone, "But Mrs. Arnett, I want it now! Now! And he will just take forever with it." Mrs. Arnett then says, "I am sorry Margo, but you will have to wait your turn. How would you like it if Luke took something you were using and refused to give it back?" Mrs. Arnett asks softly. "I dunno, I just want the green pencil back!" Margo responds as she begins to cry.

"Well, why don't we see if another group has an extra green pencil that they can share with you?" asks Mrs. Arnett. "Yes!" replies Margo immediately. With another green pencil located, the students appear to get back to work. As she makes her way back to her desk, Mrs. Arnett is happy to see most of the students on-task and hard at work. She reflects on how each year some students are so ready to come and learn, while others just need more time to adapt to the daily routines of kindergarten.

Yet she has one student, Kyle, who has again brought a toy to school in his backpack. He is not working on his illustration because he is playing with the action figure toy. Mrs. Arnett stops to remind Kyle there are no toys at school unless it is show-and-tell day, but Kyle responds that he does not want to leave the favored character by himself at home; after all, Kyle does not want him to be lonely. "How about if I take him and keep him at my desk while you work?" replies Mrs. Arnett. "Yeah! Thanks Mrs. Arnett!" replies Kyle excitedly; he then returns to his work.

Later that day, Mrs. Arnett has her teacher's aide help the students with their math lesson. She has the students grouped by their abilities, although it is difficult since what they can perform without guidance changes rapidly. Mrs. Arnett instructs Anna, her assistant, that she may help the students with their assignment, answer questions, and provide any guidance that they need; however, she is not to give them the answers nor is she to solve the problems for them.

Mrs. Arnett also instructs her to place a check mark next to the student's name indicating that she provided them with assistance on this task. Mrs. Arnett explains to Anna that the checkmarks will inform her of what the students can accomplish independently and what they needed assistance with.

This information will be beneficial to her as she begins planning the next instructional unit. In particular, she wants to reflect on the best use of small-group work to help students master the new state standards for students' mathematical learning.

As the aide begins to help students individually at their desks, Mrs. Arnett circles to help other students. She notices that one of her students, Michael, continues to have difficulty focusing on the task at hand. The teacher knows that the transition to kindergarten is a big one, and some students don't seem to adapt to life in the classroom as readily as others. Over the years, she has noted individual differences in readiness and focus on learning. She knows that given diverse preschool experiences, some kindergartners are inexperienced at working in groups and may find it hard to exercise the increasing self-discipline required in school settings.

She also considers that with ever-present electronic games and media, even for very young children, some kids struggle more than ever with those kindergarten tasks that require quieter and more focused attention. But Michael's attention span in particular is of concern, and on occasion she sees him become frustrated and overwhelmed. She walks over to offer assistance and get him back on-task. However, as she makes her way to her desk she also makes a mental note to talk with Michael's parents.

After students have left at the end of the day, Mrs. Arnett is putting away the day's materials and reflects back on her earlier experiences with the students. In addition to the individual differences in understanding and readiness for learning, she knows that some students need more help than others in learning appropriate classroom behavior including the concept of sharing and how to resolve conflicts. She knows she needs to come up with a game plan to help her students stay on-task and focused on the important learning activities she has planned for the year.

She begins to think that her upcoming math lesson on comparing length and number might help to channel conflict over "who has more" into some concrete learning opportunities. There might even be some fun homework exercises parents might get involved with to really afford students more time to practice and internalize these important mathematical concepts.

DISCUSSION QUESTIONS

1. Cognitive Development:
   a. According to Piaget, identify the stage of cognitive development that the students are likely to be in.
   b. Illustrate instances in the case which demonstrate Piaget's concept of assimilation and/or accommodation. Relate instances in the case which

demonstrate a child's schema. In particular, look to the opening of the case and the exchange between Margo and Luke.

c. Explain how Piaget's concept of egocentrism is apparent in this case. Identify strategies for how teachers can help students to appreciate the perspective of others, including their peers.

d. Discuss an instance where conservation is demonstrated by the students in this case. How do Piaget's conservation tasks link to current mathematical standards for young children like students with counting or understanding measurable attributes of objects like greater than and less than?

e. How does the incident with the action figure relate to a Piagetian notion at this stage of development?

2. Sociocultural Cognitive Development:

a. Discuss an instance in the case which involves Vygotsky's concept of the zone of proximal development.

b. Explain how scaffolding is demonstrated in this case. What are other ways this teacher might scaffold students' learning?

c. Conclude whether Mrs. Arnett is using Vygotsky's sociocontextual theory effectively in her class. Support your answer with examples from the case.

3. Psychosocial and Socioemotional Development:

a. Which stage of Erikson's stages of psychosocial development are the students likely to be in? How is that demonstrated in the case?

b. Conclude whether Mrs. Arnett is aiding her students for a positive resolution of the challenge that they experience in this stage.

c. How can teachers help students experience success in the classroom, and why is this important for their psychosocial development at these ages?

d. How can teachers recognize students' success in the classroom, and why is this important for their psychosocial development at these ages? Why is it important to emphasize a student's individual improvement at these ages?

e. How might teachers encourage appropriate social behavior, social skills, and self-control?

f. How might teachers help students develop positive relationships with their peers? How might literature and discussion help students handle the social problems typical to elementary school?

4. Classroom Management:

a. Evaluate Mrs. Arnett on her classroom management strategy. Determine her effectiveness.

b. Explain if Mrs. Arnett demonstrates "withitness" in the classroom. Support your answer with examples from the case.
c. Do you think Mrs. Arnett handled student arguments effectively? What strategies should teachers use to address students arguing in the classroom?
d. In what ways should teachers respond to students' tattling? And how might teachers respond to students who are chronic complainers?
e. What are the essential skills and routines kindergarten teachers must help students acquire? How can teachers help those students who have not adapted to the routines and rules of kindergarten given the diverse preschool experiences students come to class with?
f. How can teachers help students who struggle to focus for even short periods of learning during seatwork or small-group activities?

Case 2

When Teasing Escalates

Suggested Theories: Social Development & Bronfenbrenner's Ecological Theory, Cognitive Development, Learning Disabilities, and Classroom Management
Teacher Challenges: Peer Acceptance, Teasing, and Bullying
Student Level: Upper Elementary

As the first learning activity of the day gets underway in Mrs. Wynn's fifth-grade class, Mrs. Wynn overhears two of her students who have begun to get into a dispute. "Be quiet, Isabella," Emilia states, "it is not nice to tease others." "But it's true, Emilia—I heard you liked Deon but he doesn't like you back," teases Isabella. Isabella snickers and waits to see what Emilia will do. However, Mrs. Wynn approaches Isabella and asks, "Isabella, how do you think what you just said to Emilia made her feel?" "I dunno, Mrs. Wynn," Isabella replies as she looks toward where Emilia is sitting, "I guess, bad."

"Isabella, can you put yourself in Emilia's place and tell me how you would feel if she had said something like that to you?" Mrs. Wynn asks. Isabella is silent for a moment and then replies, "I guess I may have hurt her feelings because it isn't her fault that Deon doesn't like her." "That's right Isabella, thank you for considering the situation. You know, we all have to consider other students' feelings when deciding what to say to others." Isabella nods her head in agreement.

As Mrs. Wynn circles around the room, she reflects on the faculty meeting she recently attended on the school's implementation of peer mediators and really feels that the idea is promising. She knows that a large amount of time is often devoted to minor behavioral issues that could easily be resolved by peer mediators, while she would tackle the major discipline problems.

Mrs. Wynn also thinks that it will help students show responsibility, become more independent, and improve their social skills.

She decides to create a "corner" dedicated to the peer mediator position where she will post the descriptions for what a peer mediator would do along with a sign-up sheet encouraging her students to sign up. She also plans to have a class discussion in order to gather their thoughts and feelings on the idea.

Later in the week, Mrs. Wynn discusses peer mediators with them. After she feels her students understood the role of a mediator, she asks them to find time during learning centers to take a look at the peer mediator corner and if they are interested they are to sign up. Mrs. Wynn informs them that all of the students interested in being a peer mediator would meet with her for a few minutes before and after school in order for her to guide them on how they would solve the problems.

As students move to the learning centers they will each work at, Todd, one of Mrs. Wynn's students, thinks that this is a great idea and would like to sign up; however, he is hesitant to do so. He wants to ensure that someone from the popular crowd signs up showing this is a cool thing to do and not something that would be reserved for teachers' pets. Just as Todd is considering this issue, Jake, one of the popular boys, writes his name on the sign-up sheet. Following Jake, a few other students also sign up and lastly so does Todd.

By the end of the day, Mrs. Wynn decides to take a look at the sign-up sheet and is elated to discover that many students have indeed signed up to be peer mediators. "Wonderful! Look at all of the names on the sign-up sheet!" Mrs. Wynn exclaims excitedly as she holds up the sign-up sheet with eight names on it. "Peer mediators will be in place tomorrow and although it will be a learning process for all of us, I will begin delegating minor classroom disputes to them."

A few days later, after Mrs. Wynn has met with her peer mediators to discuss their role and has paired them off in teams of two, she believes they are ready to begin. During group assignments, the first pair of mediators has a chance to witness a dispute and to attempt to resolve it. Marshall and Dylan begin arguing over the makeup of their cooperative learning group. "Marshall," Dylan says, "I don't want you in my group. Your work is so sloppy, and you never finish your part."

Marshall is visibly upset at this accusation and responds, "Dylan, quit being so bossy, no one else cares about this stuff. It is all so boring!" Dylan replies, "Hey! You're a real pain. And no one likes you!" Before the verbal conflict can intensify, Mrs. Wynn interrupts the escalating problem and suggests that the peer mediators try to resolve the problem. Josh and Ava are the team of peer mediators that Mrs. Wynn has chosen to resolve this issue.

Mrs. Wynn asks Dylan, Marshall, Josh, and Ava to go to the mediators' corner so that they may handle the issue. "OK, let's start with each of you getting to tell your side of the story without interrupting the other person and without name-calling," says Josh. As both Dylan and Marshall each communicate what happened, Josh, Ava, and Mrs. Wynn all listen carefully. Once each has had a chance to explain, Ava asks, "OK, Dylan do you think that there was a different way in which you could have handled this situation?"

"No," Dylan replies and continues, "Marshall always pulls us down, and sometimes he doesn't even try. He just sits there doing other stuff." Josh listens to Dylan and then asks, "Well, Marshall, you definitely need to be working on the assignment that the group was given and not doing other things. Would you help your group if each of you takes turns choosing which part of the assignment you wanted to work on?" "You mean like voting?" asks Marshall. "Yes, like voting," replies Ava and continues, "that way it would be more fair."

Marshall pauses for a moment and says, "I suppose that could be better, and that way we would be doing what all of us want, not just what Dylan wants." "OK with you, Dylan?" asks Ava. "Yes, I suppose so," Dylan replies. "Great! I think we have resolved this situation. Right, Mrs. Wynn?" asks Josh excitedly. "Well, you have all done a great job; however, I did want to add that there is no need to attack a student personally when the issue is over an assignment. We can just keep the discussion to the task at hand, without any personal attacks," says Mrs. Wynn. The students all nod and then return to their seats.

As the students resume their group work, Mrs. Wynn acknowledges these concerns quite probably stem from Marshall's learning disability. Marshall is often inattentive in class, and he is constantly teased by his classmates because of his difficulties with the classwork. Normally quiet, and sometimes an anxious student, Mrs. Wynn also feels Marshall experiences more problems with social competence than other students in the classroom. Because of this, he doesn't appear to have many friends or to be well-liked either in class or during recess.

In addition, Marshall is experiencing some challenges academically, but with thirty students, it is hard for her to give him as much individual attention as he requires. She fears the problems that Marshall is having that are impeding his fitting in with his classmates are not so easily resolved.

The next day confirms her unfortunate suspicions. On the playground both boys have begun arguing about a name Dylan called Marshall. Dylan is ridiculing Marshall, and threatens that no one will like him or have him in their group in class. Once Dylan's friends seem to form around him and support him, Dylan advances toward Marshall, looking as if he might push the other student. Fearing that the verbal altercation will quickly escalate into a physical altercation, Mrs. Wynn immediately steps in and takes action to diffuse the situation.

DISCUSSION QUESTIONS

1. Social Development:

   a. From the perspective of Selman's theory of perspective taking, discuss how this theory may help students in this case become more mature. Identify strategies that Mrs. Wynn uses to aid her students in perspective taking.
   b. Explain how peers and friendship play a role in this case. From the case, can we ascertain students' peer status or peer acceptance?
   c. Relate how the different systems of Bronfenbrenner's ecological theory are apparent in this case study. Describe how the different systems are influencing social development in this case.

2. Psychosocial Development:

   a. Which stage of Erikson's stages of psychosocial development are the students likely to be in? How is that demonstrated in the case?
   b. Conclude whether the teacher is aiding her students for a positive resolution of the challenge that they experience in this stage.
   c. Discuss some of the advantages of having children take action in conflict resolution. Justify how being a peer mediator may aid in a student's development of social skills.
   d. Identify any students who may be experiencing problems with the Erikson stage that is most associated with this age group. Illustrate strategies that Mrs. Wynn might use to aid her students' successful resolution to this stage.

3. Cognitive Development:

   a. Determine how Piaget's concept of assimilation and/or accommodation is being demonstrated in the case. How does this relate to the notion of equilibrium?
   b. Identify the stage of Piaget's theory at which most of the students would be functioning in. Explain how this stage of cognitive development would have implications for reasoning ability and behavior.
   c. Evaluate how Mrs. Wynn is using Vygotsky's concept of scaffolding in the classroom.
   d. What are the most ideal ways to structure cooperative learning so students can benefit from peer scaffolding of academic concepts? Discuss the importance of the ZPD and heterogenous groups.

4. Learning Disabilities:

   a. Identify the typical symptoms associated with learning disabilities. What do you notice in Marshall's behavior?

    b. Present some teaching methods appropriate for students with a learning disability.

    c. Analyze the advantages and problems associated with labeling students.

    d. Given the age range you plan to teach, which disabilities do you feel will pose the greatest challenge for you while teaching in today's classroom?

5. Classroom Management:

    a. What happens when verbal disagreements escalate to physical aggression? How can teachers most effectively respond?

    b. How are initiatives like peer mediator programs most effectively implemented as to increase teacher's time management given the challenge teachers face in juggling multiple demands (teaching, classroom management and repetitive disturbances, assessment)?

    c. What are other ways to encourage students' independent problem-solving?

    d. When does teasing become bullying? Discuss the nature of verbal bullying (making threats, name-calling), psychological bullying (excluding children, spreading rumors), or physical bullying (hitting, pushing).

    e. What are teaching strategies to diffuse or stop bullying in the classroom? What are the elements for an effective anti-bullying school-wide program?

Case 3

Making Time for Recess

Suggested Theories: Psychosocial Development, Social Development, Cognitive Development, Moral Development, Social Cognitive Theory, and Behavioral Management
Teaching Challenges: Peer Acceptance, Peer Coaches, Recess, and Testing
Student Level: Lower Elementary

Gavin is a second grader in Ms. Burke's class at Sandy Falls Elementary. Gavin scored very high on the reading assessment given to the class and was chosen by his teacher to be a peer-coach, who assists classmates struggling to read. Using peer coaches is a strategy that his teacher first implemented a few years ago and has found to be consistently successful in helping struggling students improve while also helping peer coaches feel more competent in their reading abilities. Gavin is paired with Trevor and, at the scheduled time, Ms. Burke sends all of the students in the peer-tutor groups to Mrs. Santos, who is the library aide for peer-coach sessions.

As Gavin and Trevor are working at their table, Mrs. Santos overhears their conversation. "I hate reading. I'm never gonna be as good as you or the other peer-coach kids. I'm just no good at school!" Trevor says, exasperated. "Don't say that, Trevor. You can get better, you just have to keep working at it," Gavin responds encouragingly. "C'mon Gavin, just tell them we finished and I got them all right so we can be done. I'll give you my dessert at lunch! You're not gonna get in trouble because Ms. Burke will never know," whispers Trevor conspiratorially.

Mrs. Santos shares what she overheard with Ms. Burke, who is not pleased to hear that children who need the most assistance are not taking advantage of the extra instruction, especially since it is a challenge to find the time to implement successful instructional strategies like the peer coaches. "I am glad to hear that Gavin did not give in. I will be sure to praise him for his good decision while I speak to Trevor about his negative actions, and I will keep him out of recess again today," Ms. Burke says to Mrs. Santos, who nods her head in agreement.

Ms. Burke excuses herself to return to her class in time to see one of her students out of her seat. Ms. Burke calls out the student's name and tells her to change her color on the behavior chart. The behavior chart is located on the wall, and it contains all the students' names and their present color. The behavior system that Ms. Burke has in place is one that mirrors a traffic light, where being on green is the best and being on red the worst. Children change their color with each misbehavior, and once they reach the color red they lose recess for that day.

During a science lesson on trees later that day, Gavin is seated with his group working together to create a display on the poster board when they begin to disagree as to which pictures to include on their project board. "That isn't a tree! We can't put that on our board, we'll get it wrong! Trees don't grow all spread out and down. They grow up into the sky like the oak tree, and they only have one trunk not a bunch of them!" Stella says confidently while holding pictures of both the banyan tree and an oak tree. Gavin answers his classmate, "It's still a tree, Stella. I saw one on our vacation to Florida this summer, and it just looks different."

The other students in the group agree, but Stella still insists that her opinion is the right one. Ms. Burke shares some facts about the banyan tree in hopes of clarifying its nature to Stella, and while Stella ceases to argue, Ms. Burke doubts she's truly accepted the answer. Like Stella, there are students that cannot yet understand comparisons or differences between similar items.

Ms. Burke wishes she had more time to extend her lessons to include more discussions so students can strengthen their understanding. However, too often these discussions will run into the time reserved for another subject, and Ms. Burke finds she has to cut time from recess in order to get all that day's material covered. Soon she'll be giving her students diagnostic tests and then preparing students for state assessments.

Ms. Burke goes over to the light switch and turns the lights off and on, a signal to the students that they are to be quiet and wait for instructions. "All right everyone, it is time to clean up and get ready to go to music. Let's see which students are ready to line up," Ms. Burke says, as she looks around the room for students whose desks are cleaned as she instructed. "Looks like Gavin is definitely setting a good example, sitting quietly with his desk clean and all his belongings put away! Great job Gavin, please line up," Ms. Burke says and continues calling out other students' names.

The room is a bustle of activity as students quickly clean up their supplies, making certain their centers are all put away and then going to sit quietly so they'll be called to line up. "Uh-oh, looks like some of the students that are standing in line are not keeping their voices to a whisper like they are supposed to; it would be a shame to have to ask them to sit back down," Ms. Burke says, and suddenly the line of students by the door quickly lower their voices. However, as Ms. Burke continues to call students to line up, she has to address two students who are pushing each other.

"What is going on?" Ms. Burke asks T.J. and Evan. "I didn't push him, I tripped and, well, fell on him—but he cut the line!" T.J. says angrily. "No I didn't!" Evan replies heatedly. "There is no pushing in this classroom, and neither one of you were called to line up. Both of your desks are not cleared," Ms. Burke says firmly. "I didn't hear it was time to clean up," Evan says softly, and returns to his desk to finish cleaning up. "I was called! I heard you call me!" T.J. responds defiantly.

Ms. Burke asks both boys to move their cards to the next color and, because T.J. was disrespectful and arguing with her, he has also lost recess. T.J. is unhappy, but he does walk over and adds his name to the *NO RECESS* list. Unfortunately, Ms. Burke has come to accept that, for many of her students, it is a common practice to make excuses or lie because they think that is how they will avoid punishment.

The next day, during language arts, Ms. Burke is reviewing the concept of ABC order. After grading yesterday's quiz, she realized many students were still only alphabetizing using the first letter of a word. The class just read a story about a boy who loves to alphabetize, and therefore, Ms. Burke thinks using the story will help her students review and practice questions just like the ones on the upcoming test.

"So class, who can tell me how the boy in the story uses ABC order?" Ms. Burke asks. Ms. Burke calls on Gavin. "He doesn't just use ABC order for the first letter. If all the things have the same first letter, then he looks at the second letter, and then if the second letter is the same, he has to look at the third letter and . . . well, all the letters, until the words are all in ABC order," Gavin says. Ms. Burke responds, "That's correct! Gavin, please come up to the board and demonstrate for us by completing the problem on the whiteboard." Gavin walks up and correctly alphabetizes the list. He writes: *Beast, Beautiful, Being, Bell, Bench, Bent, Best*.

"OK T.J., please come up and complete the next set," Ms. Burke says. "Oh, but Ms. Burke, I have so many more words to do than Gavin had," T.J. whines, pointing to the words. Ms. Burke realizes that while there is the same amount of words on the board for T.J. to complete, the seven words are spread out more across the board—and thus appear to T.J. as being a longer list. Ms. Burke rewrites the list to match the list that Gavin had and shows T.J. that the list just looked differently but there are still seven words. T.J. nods happily and gets to work.

As the lesson continues, Ms. Burke can see that students like Evan who had incorrectly understood ABC order can now complete the task correctly; however, students like Carmen are still not alphabetizing beyond the first letter unless they are assisted. It is clear to her that some of these students are struggling with feeling competent and that some will act out in frustration at their lack of ability. That was certainly the case with Stella when she said the words were stupid after not being able put them in ABC order.

Then, when Ms. Burke asked her to change her card for her outburst she refused because she argued she hadn't done anything wrong, and that Ms. Burke was mean and just did not like her. Stella lost recess for that day. Ms. Burke ends the lesson saying, "Remember class, practice the worksheets I am sending home for homework tonight, as well as the page numbers you wrote on your agendas. Both have questions that are exactly like the ones on the test." Ms. Burke doesn't like teaching to the test, but she is unsure of what else she can do so that all her students learn the standards she is required to test them on.

As the class is getting ready to go out for recess, Ms. Burke observes that there is a large number of students who will be sitting out of recess today. While it is certainly an improvement over last week, it is still likely to be a challenging afternoon since many students will not have a chance to burn off excess energy. After all, her students do not have physical education every day and without recess they will have to go the entire school day without the chance to exercise their bodies, and it will likely affect their attention span and concentration.

At recess that day, Ms. Burke is watching her students play. The group closest to her is enjoying role-playing as they enact characters from a TV show she knows is a favorite of her students. "You be the super-secret spy, Gavin, that has superhero powers!" shouts one of the other students playfully. "OK, and you be the hawk that transforms into the powerful dragon!" Gavin replies excitedly. Ms. Burke sees many of her students playing with children in other second-grade classes. They are playing a made-up game with a ball.

However, one of her students, Carmen, is walking over to her with tears in her eyes and says, "Ms. Burke, those girls are not letting me play and I tried to do what you always tell us, you know, talk and come up with a solution. But, they won't let me in their special best friend club. They say only kids they choose can be in it." Ms. Burke nods her head empathetically and goes over, speaks to all of the girls, but while she reminds them to consider other's feelings when playing, she knows that exclusion from peer groups happens frequently.

Unfortunately, it often is the same kids that get left out and have trouble making friends. Ms. Burke hopes her intervention will work; she knows that consistently encountering social challenges will also affect a student's learn-ing, especially one who is already struggling academically.

DISCUSSION QUESTIONS

1. Psychosocial Development:

   a. Which stage of Erikson's stages of psychosocial development are the students likely to be in? How is that demonstrated in the case?
   b. Conclude whether Ms. Burke is aiding her students for a positive reso-lution of the challenge that they experience in this stage.
   c. How can teachers help students experience competency in the class-room, and why is this important for their psychosocial development at these ages?
   d. What strategies did Ms. Burke employ that can enhance a student's sense of industry in this case? What other strategies could also promote success?
   e. How can teachers recognize students' success in the classroom, and how is that linked to the child's psychosocial development in this stage?
   f. Define the concept of inferiority complex. Discuss how students develop an inferiority complex. What strategies can a teacher employ that help to reduce inferiority in their students?
   g. How does Ms. Burke's peer-coach strategy assist students with indus-try? Generate other instructional strategies that assist in the develop-ment of industry.

2. Socioemotional Development:

   a. Discuss how the teacher in this case tackled social problems that were occurring in her class. How would her approach to allow students to handle conflict and solve their own problems lead to better social development? How could it exacerbate the problem?
   b. How might teachers encourage appropriate social behavior, social skills, and empathy in this age of students? How can teachers help prevent the exclusion of some children in others' social play?
   c. How might teachers lead large group discussions with their students in how to develop and maintain positive relationships with their peers in this age of student?
   d. From the perspective of Selman's theory of perspective taking, discuss how this theory may help students in this case become more mature.

Identify strategies that Ms. Burke uses to aid her students in perspective taking.

e. Explain how peers and friendship play a role in this case. From the case, can we ascertain students' peer status or peer acceptance?

f. Outline which of the different systems of Bronfenbrenner's ecological theory are apparent in this case. Describe how the different systems are influencing social development in this case.

g. Discuss the importance of recess for school age children. What is the goal of recess? What needs does it serve in children of this age group? How does cutting recess affect a child's social development? Should recess be mandatory?

3. Cognitive Development:

a. According to Piaget, identify the stage of cognitive development that the students are likely to be in.

b. Illustrate instances in the case which demonstrate Piaget's concept of assimilation that is taking place in the case.

c. Illustrate instances in the case which demonstrate Piaget's concept of accommodation that is taking place in the case.

d. Identify an example in the case where Piaget's concept of egocentrism is clearly demonstrated.

e. Explain Piaget's concept of schema and identify the schemas that are apparent in this case. Identify strategies for how teachers can help students develop and extend their schemas.

f. Outline various ways that children's experiences shape their schemas and affect their assimilations and accommodations.

g. Discuss the concept of equilibration, and discuss if in Stella's case the entire process took place. How can teachers assist students to regain equilibrium?

h. Explain the Piagetian concept that is being demonstrated when T.J. thinks that the list of words that he has to work on the board is longer simply because it is written differently.

4. Moral Development:

a. According to Kohlberg's theory of moral development, determine the level and stage that Trevor is exhibiting in this case. Discuss examples in the case that speak to his reasoning at the level and stage chosen.

b. According to Kohlberg's theory of moral development, determine the level and stage that other students in the class are exhibiting. Support your answer with examples from the case.

c. How can Ms. Burke tackle the moral issues of lying, making up excuses, and bargaining with others in her classroom to promote better moral development in her students?

    d. According to Piaget's theory of moral development, discuss the stage that the students in the case are functioning in. How is that indicative in their actions in the case?

    e. According to Piaget's theory of moral development, discuss the stage that the students in the case are functioning in. How is that indicative in their actions in the case?

5. Behavioral Approaches and Classroom Management:

    a. How is the teachers' use of the behavior chart an example of behavior management? Discuss its effectiveness.

    b. Identify the teachers' classroom management strategy. How is that evident in the case?

    c. How does consistently removing recess prove to be an ineffective punishment? What other punishments could the teacher in the case use that could prove effective in curbing misbehavior?

    d. In general, what are the disadvantages of using punishment in the classroom?

    e. Identify examples of positive reinforcement found in the case. What type of positive reinforcement is the teacher employing? Discuss the advantages and disadvantages of using intrinsic and extrinsic reinforcers in the classroom.

    f. Explain examples found in the case of negative reinforcement. Discuss the teacher's effectiveness at using negative reinforcement.

    g. Discuss how Ms. Burke uses signals to help students' transition. How is that an effective part of her classroom management routine?

    h. How is the teachers' concern for meeting state standards for curriculum interfering with her teaching methods? How is it affecting the strategies she chooses?

6. Social Cognitive Theory;

    a. How does Ms. Burke employ observational learning and vicarious consequences in her classroom? Discuss the teacher's effectiveness using examples from the case.

    b. Discuss the concept of self-efficacy. How does self-efficacy develop? How does self-efficacy play a role in children's academic success? How does a sense of competence relate to success? Discuss Gavin's self-efficacy in comparison to the children who are struggling.

    c. Outline what self-regulation is and how it affects learning and achievement. How are self-regulation and self-efficacy related? Speculate how children who possess industry would be more likely to be self-regulated.

Case 4

Cheating in the Technology Age

Suggested Theories: Moral Development, Cognitive Development, Social Development, and Parental Involvement
Teacher Challenges: Cheating, Helicopter Parenting, and Technology in the Classroom
Student Level: Upper Elementary

Dana Callaghan is a new fourth-grade teacher at Washington Elementary. As she gets ready for her students to arrive, she runs into Gary Howard, one of the retired teachers who work in aftercare. "Good morning Dana, do you have a few minutes?" Gary asks. "Sure, Gary!" Dana exclaims. Gary smiles and says, "Well, I wanted to share with you some of the things I noticed happening in aftercare with some of your students. While I don't know the nature of your assignments or the policies you have in place for them on how they are to complete their homework, it looks to me like many are sharing their answers."

Gary continues, "Especially when they are in the technology lab, they cut and paste most of the information. However, when I asked them, they said that they were helping each other, not copying. I have also noticed that many ask older children to help which leads to the older kids completing the work for them. I even find myself reducing the amount of assistance I provide, because I feel that many are looking for me to do it for them, so they can say they are finished and go and play." Dana responds surprised, "I truly had no idea this was happening! Thanks, Gary."

"Well I think that kids will always try to test the boundaries between what is right and what is wrong, but it is the frequency of the occurrences, as well as the number of students doing it, that had me wanting to share this with

23

you," Gary says as he and Dana say their goodbyes, and Dana's students begin entering the classroom.

Later that day, Dana is checking each student's individual progress on their Native-American projects, and she notices that the wording in a student's project is too advanced and doubts that the student wrote it herself. In fact, she suspects that her work was directly cut and pasted from one of her sources. She asks the student to come to her desk to discuss privately with her. "Adrianna, some of these words are very advanced. For example, you have here that this tribe was a *cognate tribe that is loosely aligned with other tribes of that region,* can you please tell me what that means?" Dana asks, pointing to the section in Adrianna's summary.

"Hmm, I am not sure I guess what they are . . . umm." Adrianna trails off without finishing. Mrs. Callaghan asks, "Why don't you show me the notes you took when you were researching the websites for your project? Perhaps that will help you remember?" "I don't have any notes, I mean, I didn't know we had to have notes, I . . . umm, just put it all into my summary," Adrianna says, stammering. "Adrianna, your summary has to be written in your own words as we discussed in class. Remember that when you present your work you will need to show you know it," Dana says.

Dana goes over the project's rubric with Adrianna again, and she highlights the portions about putting research into their own words to ensure that the directions are clear. Adrianna shares that she sees her mother cut and paste recipes off the internet all of the time, and that her dad cuts and pastes order numbers in order to save time and maximize production when he works at home. It is clear, as Dana continues checking her students' work, that Adrianna is not the only one who is cutting and pasting from websites.

Dana mulls this over. Is it possible that her students do not truly understand the severity of their actions? That they do not understand that what they are doing constitutes cheating? Being that we live in a technology-driven world where shortcuts are taken easily in order to increase efficiency and productivity, is it possible they do not realize that cutting and pasting numbers or a recipe is not the same as using others words as your own? Are they too young to understand that we have to give credit to the author of the work?

Later that day, Dana overhears the group adjacent to the one she is working with discuss the educational game that they are playing on the schools' iPads. Much to Dana's dismay she realizes that the girls are sharing answers! Dana wonders how many other students have been doing this! The educational app sends Dana a diagnostic report of each student's progress; however, being that they are sharing answers she questions not only the validity of the tool for formative assessment but also the effectiveness of the educational app itself. The girls make plans to contact each other after school.

It seems that Lacy has a sitter that watches her and her siblings while her parents work, and this sitter who is a high schooler has taught her a few tricks to get homework done quicker. "Yeah, the sitter showed me how to open multiple windows on the computer. Then we logged in to my little brother's learning site for his homework using my username and password from last year—the answers are all still there! We opened a new window, logged him in, and copied all the answers. We were done so fast that we got to play in the pool all afternoon! It was awesome!" Lacy says excitedly.

"Wow! You think she'll help us with our homework tonight again?" Ashley asks. "Sure! She doesn't mind. I'll just log into my sisters' iPad and we can video chat! I know where she keeps her password to get into her iPad," Lacy says. "Wait," Octavia, a student who had silently been listening to the girls' conversation, interrupts and asks, "Does your sister know that you are using her iPad?"

Lacy giggles and says, "Nope, she has no clue!" Octavia says "But, I mean, that's wrong. Wouldn't she be mad if she found out? And your parents, wouldn't they get mad if they heard your little brother is not really doing his math work?" Lacy frowns and she and Ashley roll their eyes. "Well they might be mad, Octavia, but no one is going to tell them because we are all friends, right?" Lacy says annoyed. "Friends keep each other's secrets. Lacy and I thought you were cool like us. You're not going to be uncool today when you're at my house right? You do want to be our friend right?" Ashley asks. Octavia quickly says, "No, of course, I want to come over. I'm your friend. I love coming over your house when my mom works late." Dana is concerned by what she overhears. Lacy's sitter is negatively influencing her, and she and Ashley are pressuring Octavia to accept a situation that she doesn't seem comfortable with in the name of friendship.

Later in the week, the class is reviewing for their upcoming math test and Dana notices that some of the students are repeatedly making mistakes when coming up to the whiteboard to solve problems. Similarly, in her "speed review" where she calls out a problem and students write the answers on their individual whiteboards and show it to her, she notices that there are a number of students getting the wrong answers. This is surprising to her as homework grades and take-home quizzes all demonstrated that the students had a good grasp on the material.

As the students play in recess, she chats about the upcoming test with the students that are closest to her. "So are you all ready for your test?" Dana asks the group. Hector says "Not sure Mrs. Callaghan, hope it's not too hard." "Hector, what happened today during math review? I saw you were struggling but your homework was excellent all week as was your take-home quiz," Dana asks.

Hector answers, "I guess I wasn't paying close attention when my dad was doing it at home. He is really good at math and gets frustrated when I don't get it because he doesn't want me to fail, so he tells me the answer so I don't get it wrong. My older sister does the same thing, because if not I would get really bad grades on homework."

Hector runs away to join his friends on the playground, but leaves Dana to wonder about the amount of assistance some of her students are getting at home. If her students are getting too much assistance from parents, older siblings, or more knowledgeable peers, it would undoubtedly explain the discrepancy in scores she is noticing between students' take-home assignments and their in-class assignments. This information also ties in with her earlier conversation with Gary about what he had noticed in aftercare.

On Friday of that week, it is a teacher's professional day and Dana decides to approach her colleague for advice. Mariaelisa is a veteran fifth-grade teacher whose classroom is across the hall. "Hi Mariaelisa, you have time to chat?" Dana asks. "Oh, hey Dana, sure, come on in! How's it going? How are you adjusting?" Mariaelisa asks cheerfully as Dana sits on a chair opposite from her. "Good, thanks, I am enjoying teaching fourth grade even if I had thought I would be teaching first grade," Dana replies sincerely. "Great! I've heard parents compliment your teaching methods and your students really like you," Mariaelisa replies warmly.

Dana thanks her, and shares issues that recently surfaced in her classroom, as well as what Gary revealed about aftercare. "Well I am certainly not surprised by what you are telling me, and I have encountered similar issues to the ones you are dealing with in the past. I think that because technology is a daily part of our students' lives, their actions on the internet may not always relate directly in their minds to how they have defined cheating or plagiarism. I believe that has to be explicitly taught, especially since these students are concrete learners, and thus their understanding is more rigid and grounded in tangible realities," Mariaelisa says thoughtfully.

Dana nods her head and says, "I fully agree, it's what I was thinking as well. However, I was unsure of how teachers should approach moral issues and certainly wouldn't want to interfere with parental beliefs." Mariaelisa replies, "I have always believed that as long as the moral concerns we are discussing with our students apply to the classroom, such as cheating and plagiarism, which are part of school rules then we are doing them a benefit to help them firmly establish a moral foundation."

Mariaelisa continues, "Unfortunately, parents are not always vigilant to this behavior at home or often believe that elementary-age children are too young to receive harsh punishments for cheating or plagiarism." Dana nods in agreement. Mariaelisa continues, "Have you ever heard of the term 'helicopter parents'?" Dana says she hasn't. So Mariaelisa explains, "Well it refers to parents that give too much help to their kids because they do not want them to struggle or risk failure. The result is the child performs excellently on homework but not on classwork."

"That sounds like what I am encountering with some of the parents in my class," Dana agrees, surprised. Their conversation then moves to discussing the benefits of using educational apps in the classroom when Dana shares what she discovered with Ashley. Both teachers agree that some educational apps are beneficial and enhance students' learning, others are not. Therefore, teachers are faced with the daunting task of selecting the most proven apps from the wide array of apps available on the market today. After her talk with her colleague, Dana decides that she is going to have a discussion with her students that explicitly covers these recent issues.

DISCUSSION QUESTIONS

1. Moral Development:
   a. According to Kohlberg's theory of moral development, determine the level and stage that the students in this class are exhibiting. Discuss examples from the case that demonstrate that.
   b. From the perspective of Kohlberg's theory of moral development, discuss how Octavia's progression to the next stage in moral development may be slower due to fear of her friends isolating her or upsetting girls she wants to be friends with.
   c. At what age should moral discussions take place in education? Why is it important for students in elementary school to understand concepts like plagiarism and intellectual property? What future problems could establishing a moral foundation prevent for the future?
   d. Discuss how Lacy and Ashley are behaving in ways that are not morally correct. How is Lacy's babysitter contributing to her lack of understanding of moral concepts? How is she teaching her to take shortcuts that Lacy may then generalize to all classroom situations?
   e. The teacher in this case is faced with many moral issues that she decides need to be handled. Identify other moral dilemmas that may plague teachers of young children. What strategies can teachers use when discussing issues of a moral nature with their class?
   f. Speculate on the importance of collaboration among teachers and for a school-wide mentor program that offers new teachers strategies and assistance in navigating their new jobs.

2. Socioemotional Development and Parental Involvement:

   a. Explain how peers play a role in this case. Although these children are young, is there evidence of a clique? Discuss the influence of peer pressure and acceptance that plays a role in Octavia's behavior.
   b. Speculate how their friendships can be affected by their involvement in social media and how this may shape an adolescents' social development.
   c. Discuss how you could apply Bronfenbrenner's ecological systems theory to this case. Which of Bronfenbrenner's ecological systems would be most influential in this case?
   d. Parent involvement is crucial for academic success; however, when does parenting involvement become a problem?
   e. Discuss the notion of "helicopter parenting." What negative effects does it have for children's learning and achievement? How can parenting styles impact a child's behavior—both academically and socially?
   f. Outline strategies that may best serve teachers who have to discuss "helicopter parenting" with their students' parents or guardians.

3. Cognitive Development:

   a. What stage of Piaget's theory of cognitive development are the students in this case functioning in? Support with examples from the case.
   b. Discuss how their stage of cognitive development could be linked to their moral decisions and their moral reasoning.
   c. What problems may concrete thinkers encounter when faced with abstract concepts that require reasoning beyond their stage of cognitive development? How can teachers assist students to overcome difficulties when faced with abstract concepts such as what constitutes cheating at this age?
   d. Discuss the role that social media may play in children's cognitive development? How could social media impede rather than assist a student's cognitive growth?
   e. How can a child's schema be affected due to information and experiences that they are exposed to? In this case, address this question with reference to Lacy and her babysitter.
   f. How can forming an incorrect schema of a concept affect future assimilations and accommodations? Address this question in reference to Lacy.

4. Technology in the Classroom:

   a. There are many educational apps, websites, and programs designed to help kids learn; however, what issues do the students in the case bring to light that contradicts this?

b. How can teachers ensure that they are using educational programs and apps that are truly assisting learning?

c. Discuss some of the dangers that can exist when students learn to cheat the system or to use loopholes to complete work on educational sites. How might that knowledge of shortcuts and loopholes extend to classroom work?

d. At what grade levels should teachers begin introducing students to the idea of internet plagiarism and intellectual ownership?

e. Generate strategies or tactics that teachers can employ in discussing technology with their students.

f. What information can schools disseminate to parents to keep them abreast of the types of the detriments that leaving children unsupervised on websites can have on education and achievement?

Part II

INDIVIDUAL DIFFERENCES
AND DIVERSITY

Case 5

Identifying Gifted Learners

Suggested Theories: Intelligence, Students Who Are Gifted and Talented, Cultural and Ethnic Diversity in Gifted Education, and Parent Involvement
Teacher Challenges: Identifying and Teaching Gifted Students, Instructional Pacing and Differentiated Instruction, Grouping Strategies, and Effective Communication with Parents
Student Level: Early Elementary

Camila, a first-grader in Mrs. Isabel Burton's class at Eisenhower Elementary School, is seated at the assisted reading table where Mrs. Burton guides a small group of students through a story by asking a series of questions that promote literacy understanding. This is Camila's first time at the assisted reading table. Although she has heard other students talk about this activity, and has observed it from afar while involved in other activities, she wonders if she will enjoy it. Brittney, Elijah, and Mason are also new at assisted reading, for Mrs. Burton chose groups at random and this will be the last group to engage in this activity.

Mrs. Burton soon joins the group, explains the activity, asks if there are any questions, and then begins the story. As the assisted reading activity is taking place, Mrs. Burton notices that not only are Camila and Mason answering all of the questions correctly, but they are doing so considerably faster than the other two students in the group. They are also understanding the relationships among words found in the lesson and comprehending the meaning of the exercises at a quicker pace.

As the students approach the end of the assisted reading activity, Mrs. Burton is mentally noting that grouping these students as she has done was not beneficial for this lesson, for there were too many challenges with regard to the students' individual progress. She has always known that not all students learn at the same pace, but she is surprised by how quickly Camila and Mason are grasping the lesson. She wonders if the particular story she chose captured their interest. Or was it the composition of the group? Because she knows these students all get along well. She notes she may need to make changes with regard to the next assisted reading lesson.

The following day, Mrs. Burton begins a lesson where the students sit in a circle while they practice their spelling words. Mrs. Burton calls out the spelling word and beginning with the student closest to her, they each call out the letter that comes next in the word. If you call out the wrong letter, then you are out and you simply remove yourself from the circle; the students that are still in the circle when the lesson ends win a prize.

As the lesson begins, the students are all eagerly participating, all except for Mason that is. Mason is participating, but Mrs. Burton thinks he is lacking enthusiasm, in fact, he looks rather bored. Yet, Mrs. Burton notices that despite his lack of interest, Mason has yet to miss a letter, even when he does not look like he is even paying attention. The lesson finishes with Camila and Mason as the winners of the spelling lesson. As students move to get into their groups, Mrs. Burton makes her way to Camila's group.

"Mason, did you enjoy the spelling task?" Mrs. Burton asks. "Um, no, because I already knew the words for this week; my mom and I usually spell harder words at home. I am so good at spelling. I am the best speller ever!" Mason exclaims proudly. "Well, I am so glad that you like to spell and that your mom helps you." She turns to Camila, "What about the assisted reading activity yesterday? Did you like that?" Mrs. Burton asks. "Yes, it was fun because I never heard of that book before and it had a funny ending. But you know what would have been even funnier is if you did not see it coming—you know, if it was a surprise," Camila replies.

"Really? I am surprised that you did not say that during the session?" Mrs. Burton asks. "Well, they are my friends and, um, well, I did not know if they saw it too or not, and so um, I don't want to be a know-it-all," Camila says with a small smile. Mrs. Burton's attention is diverted to another student, and then she awards the prizes and the students are directed to get ready for physical education.

Later that day, the class begins their math lesson using different geometric shapes in helping them to identify the attributes of each shape. Mrs. Burton explains the instructions, pairs the students into groups of two, and then the students begin their work. As Mrs. Burton moves around the pairs of students, she observes how Regina, the student paired with Mason, seems to be the only one in the pair to be using the manipulatives. In fact, when Mrs. Burton looks at Mason's paper, he has already answered most of the questions, and at a quick glance, Mrs. Burton confirms that they are all correct.

"Mason, are you using the shapes to answer your questions?" Mrs. Burton asks taking the student aside. "Yeah," Mason responds. "Well, I could not help but notice that you have answered questions on the octagon, and that shape has not reached this side of the room yet," Mrs. Burton says, as she points to where the octagon is and continues, "See, Melissa and Niya are still working with it."

Mason seems irritated and quickly asks if he is in trouble for not using the shapes. Mrs. Burton immediately clarifies by explaining to him that she just wants to know as much as she can about each student and how they are learning the lessons she assigns. Mason seems somewhat relieved, and then tells her that he did not need to use them. In fact, Mrs. Burton recalls a similar instance that occurred when the class was using different manipulatives to solve addition and subtraction problems.

Neither Mason nor Camila seemed to need the manipulatives to arrive at the correct responses, although after being teased by fellow classmates, both students handled the shapes. Camila seemed to be worried and was especially sensitive to how the other students in the group reacted. However, Mason had actually received a verbal reprimand for using the shapes incorrectly, since he and another student had used the shapes as building blocks they would stack and knock down. Mason became angry when he told Mrs. Burton that he didn't understand why he couldn't play with the shapes if he was done with his work and had gotten his answers right.

On Friday, during a teacher work day, Isabel is busy incorporating new information into her future lessons and considering giving more enrichment activities to both Mason and Camila. Her colleague, Kyle, a second-grade teacher, has just stopped by her classroom upon his return from lunch. His classroom is located next to Isabel's, and since this is Isabel's first year teaching, she has often called upon him for assistance with general questions, paperwork, and the like. He has been very helpful during her adjustment period. "So Isabel, how are your students treating you?" Kyle asks in a friendly tone.

"Well, things have been going great, they respond very well to my lessons, are excited about getting to work, and for the most part are all completing all of their assignments. However, I do have two students that I have been thinking about often. They are completing work faster than I can assign it, and I sometimes feel like I may not be challenging them. It's possible that these students might be gifted. Unless I missed them, I haven't seen any test scores in their files, but it would certainly explain many of the behaviors I am observing," Isabel states.

"You should certainly pursue this with our ESE coordinator to double-check, and if not, see what you can do about beginning the evaluation process," Kyle offers. "One other thought, I know in the past you have mentioned that you like to randomly group students. I know some people still firmly believe in grouping students by ability, but others have moved on to more mixed-ability groups. I am not sure what camp you are in, and

I certainly don't want to step on your toes, but you might consider alternative grouping strategies," Kyle finishes.

Isabel continues, "So true, I have already made a note to rethink my groups. There also seems to be a big difference in their home lives, though, that I have noted. One students' family seems to be very supportive of his education, while the other student's family is almost the opposite," Isabel says. "Really? How so?" asks Kyle listening attentively. "Well, for example, the class had projects to involve their families in helping them decorate a picture I gave them after reading one of our books. Mason's family created a wonderful picture with many different materials and colors."

Kyle smiles and Isabel continues, "Mason told me how his mom had made a trip to the local craft store with him to allow him to choose the items he would use to decorate the picture, and the finished product included his entire family's input. In fact, Mason's mother has already been in touch with me about the possibility of Mason being gifted. She says she has already had Mason tested and tried to advocate on his behalf in kindergarten to be moved into a gifted class. But something fell through, and he was not accepted for the placement."

Kyle nods, as Isabel says, "I know she has reached out to the ESE coordinator, Ms. Rawlings, on numerous occasions. I will have to get back to her soon now that I have seen how well Mason is doing. But I will admit I am a little hesitant, as his mom is quite the advocate! She is very persistent and willing to pursue extra tutoring if it means getting Mason into the gifted program. However, Camila, who comes from a large Hispanic family, did all of the work by herself with what she could find around the house because she told me her mom was busy attending to company."

Isabel smiles as she continues, "Her picture was excellent! She has also told me that there are four children in total, and her house is always very busy. Camila's mother is actually a lovely woman, but upon chatting with her informally one day, I learned that she doesn't want to admit to one of her children's school work being better than the other. She said that she knew her other kids were jealous of Camila, and in response, she always tried to downplay any attention she received because she did not want jealousy issues."

Isabel then tells Kyle, "Camila's mom proceeded to tell me how all of the other children like to watch television and are actively engaged in sports, and while Camila is involved in sports, reading is her passion and she is really imaginative and more into creative types of fun. Camila's mother also appreciated that Camila tried to keep the peace at home and accepted more responsibilities like helping watch her younger siblings or helping them with their homework."

Kyle nods for her to continue. "Camila's mom explained she did not know why Camila was so different from her siblings, because, after all, they were all siblings. And considering all this, especially in light of some of Camila's reactions in class, I get the feeling that Camila is beginning to be ashamed of her differences in ability and will actively hide her differences in order to be liked and avoid ridicule. Kyle, I guess I am looking for ways to help these students in the classroom and perhaps in the process how to effectively work with their parents," Isabel says.

"In particular," Isabel continues, "I know many have discussed how we must work on better identifying Hispanic and other non-White students in programs that serve the gifted and talented." Kyle nods his head in agreement before he adds, "And don't forget about Mason, I have seen what happens when gifted students are not identified. They can become bored or frustrated with the instruction that is not paced to their individual needs."

"Or," Kyle adds, "they become accustomed to a more relaxed approach to learning, are not challenged to grow academically, and develop poor work habits which become problematic when they do eventually face difficulty with more demanding and complex subject matter. It really is a critical issue we have to address. Are we effectively identifying and teaching our gifted students?"

DISCUSSION QUESTIONS

1. Intelligence:
   a. Discuss what intelligence means. Address the debate of intelligence being composed of one ability versus many abilities.
   b. Compare and contrast fluid vs. crystallized intelligence.
   c. Differentiate between Sternberg's triarchic theory of intelligence, and Gardner's theory of multiple intelligences. What implications do these intelligence theories pose for the classroom?
   d. How is intelligence most commonly measured? Discuss the origins of IQ. Summarize how IQ scores are distributed in the population. What is the bell-shaped curve with regard to IQ scores?
   e. Describe the nature-nurture debate as it pertains to intelligence.
   f. In this case, we see examples of how Camila and Mason differ from other students with regard to classroom performance. What relationship does intelligence have with achievement?
   g. Camila's mother is making a case for her desire that all of her children be more similar with respect to achievement, what relationship exists between intelligence and heredity? Intelligence and environment?

2. Identifying the Gifted and Talented:
   a. Describe what it means to be gifted. Generate the characteristics that Camila and Mason are exhibiting that would be most consistent with

being gifted. What other gifted student characteristics exist that are not demonstrated in this case?

b. During what ages are students usually identified as being gifted? Discuss the role of the general educator and the parent. What are the main criteria for a student's placement in a gifted classroom?

c. Are there any gender differences in how gifted students may react to their relative high ability? Is one gender more likely to try and hide their giftedness to avoid standing out or from having a negative impact on their social relationships? Do gifted boys and girls have different coping mechanisms to handle their gifted abilities?

d. What cultural differences exist in how we identify students who are gifted? How can educational stakeholders work to ensure assessment and evaluation is improved to identify gifted students across demographic groups, as well as find appropriate educational placement.

e. What does the phrase "twice exceptional" refer to? What are the special learning needs of gifted students with learning disabilities?

3. Gifted Education:

a. What does the nature of gifted education look like today? Outline teaching strategies for gifted children. Compare and contrast between acceleration and enrichment, with regard to gifted education.

b. Explain examples of modifications that can be infused to regular instruction to account for students whom are gifted. In particular, discuss impact of individualized instruction or differentiated instruction.

c. Compare and contrast different approaches to grouping students including ability grouping, heterogenous or mixed-ability grouping, as well as cross-age grouping. What is flexible grouping and how does it fit in with more adaptive teaching?

d. Discuss the ramifications of students who are not accurately identified and placed in gifted programs. Specifically, what are the negative consequences for academic motivation, unhealthy work habits, and classroom management?

e. What national guidelines exist for teachers' professional development in gifted education? What is gifted endorsement?

4. Parent Involvement:

a. Devise suggestions that you would give the teacher for how to handle issues of intelligence with her students' parents.

b. Evaluate how teachers should best communicate with parents and families as educational partners on this issue.

c. What role does a parent play in identifying their child's special needs? Discuss the importance of parental advocacy and parental consent.

d. Summarize ideas of how parents and teachers can work together to ensure that a child's educational needs are being met.
e. What special challenges do parents with gifted children experience in keeping them challenged? What are the risks of a hyper-focus on academics for young students identified as being gifted?

Case 6

The Changing Views
on Students' Intelligence

Suggested Theories: Emotional Intelligence, Multiple Intelligences, Successful Intelligence, and Constructivist Teaching

Teacher Challenges: Changing Perspectives on Intelligence, Differing Learning Preferences, Managing Conflict in the Classroom, and Student Challenges with Independent Learning

Student Level: Elementary

Matthew Corby and Eileen Hamilton are third-grade co-teachers with considerable teaching experience. Known for being pioneers in tackling new teaching initiatives, they have begun a new team-teaching quest of incorporating more engaging, authentic, and differentiated instruction into their classrooms. They have decided on the use of learning centers to be the most obvious approach to exposing children to diverse learning opportunities that speak to their unique talents and learning approaches.

After many cups of coffee and several hours of work, they have created the idea of differentiated learning centers. These centers employ different levels of content and skill, and afford teachers the opportunity to observe and monitor students' learning needs. Matthew and Eileen, like many other teachers in their school, join forces when teaching some units to their classes and bring classes together in a collaborative effort.

"Students, I can't tell you how excited I am that we are beginning our new unit on the rain forest," says Mr. Corby. "Not only am I excited about the rain forest, I am excited about how we are going to be learning about the rain forest. This is something new we have never done before, and I am sure you are going to be as thrilled as I am." He waits a moment to allow the momentum of excitement to dawn on students' faces before continuing.

"We are going to be learning about the human, plant, and animal life that make their homes in the rain forest through fun learning center activities. Take a look around the room. See the different stations we have set up with lots of interesting materials? Not only are you going to read about the rain forest in books, you are going to be able to see, hear, and feel what the rain forest is like! We are even going to be learning about some of the threats to the rain forest! And best of all, we will be joined by Mrs. Hamilton's class for this activity!" Mr. Corby motions to Mrs. Hamilton's class who have arrived by the back door of the large science lab classroom.

Many students begin to shift excitedly in their seats and some begin to stand up in anticipation. However, the teachers also notice that some of the students' eyes are wide with confusion and begin to look about to see if anyone else is as dismayed as they are. Some have begun to give each other "high-fives" and are talking excitedly with each other, and some students are seen trying to look over to the centers in an attempt to have their first crack at the learning centers. A student named Reginald is immediately interested: "All right! I'm ready, when do we choose?" Several other students agree with a vigorous shaking of their heads.

"Well, Reginald, that is our first order of business." Mr. Corby replies. As the teachers go through the motions of calling students by note card, they ask each student to pick up their assigned folder to chart their progress and attendance at each of the learning centers. As students are called, they begin to make their way to a self-selected learning center. Mr. Corby assures students that getting to choose first will be random and that everyone will have a chance to pick first at some point.

After all students are working at a learning center, the teachers begin to move around the classroom to observe students and help out where necessary. Mrs. Hamilton makes a beeline for some of the students she witnessed who were less than pleased about the ideas of learning centers. "Julie, how is it going? I see you chose the practical and applied center focused on threats to the rainforest." Julie smiles, but then returns her questioning look with nothing shy of bewilderment. She then waves her hand across the multitude of materials at this particular station, "Well, Mrs. Hamilton, I don't know where to begin! What am I supposed to be doing?"

Mrs. Hamilton smiles patiently and replies, "Julie, how about these maps of some of the rainforests in South America? Or these charts of some of the endangered species that make their home there? Then there are some neat pictures taken in the rainforests. You can even follow along with some of the outlines of ideas proposed to respond to threats to the rainforest."

Once Julie is on-track and engaged with various pictures of endangered animals and deforestation, Mrs. Hamilton makes her way to other students.

She stops momentarily at two of her own students, Avery and Lance, who are making their way through the interpersonal station on the native people of the rainforest that includes a cooperative worksheet activity. The boys are working in pairs to learn various facts on how native people depend on the rainforest for shelter, food, and medicine when they begin to argue about their answers. Since the boys seem to be having trouble managing the conflict, Mrs. Hamilton moves in quickly to provide assistance.

"What are you talking about?" Lance asks, clearly frustrated and quickly becoming angry. "I keep telling you this over and over again, you can't put that down as an answer." Avery responds without waiting for Lance to finish, "I know, I know! You have said that a thousand times." At this point Mrs. Hamilton interjects, "Why hello, Lance and Avery, I see you are passionate about this topic. How can I help out here?" and she tries to help them resolve the argument.

After having squelched the conflict, she continues to circulate about the learning stations. She wonders how two students such as Lance and Avery can do so well on traditional types of testing, and yet struggle with such an activity as this current one. She watches as Mr. Corby also circulates among the student groups and is interacting with them in a very animated fashion, clearly enjoying the class activity. He is currently working with Chen, who is thoroughly absorbed in his work at the KWL intrapersonal station designed to track what the student knows (K), wants to know (W), and has learned (L) about a topic.

Mr. Corby is helping Chen finish his goal-setting sheet to chart his learning and begin to fill out the checklist of his personal interest inventory in aspects of the rainforest. He then makes his way to Mrs. Hamilton and begins to communicate his excitement, "I can't believe how well this is going! I just finished working with Chen at the KWL center, and he is getting so much out of it! Talk about emotional intelligence! I also can't get over another group's progress in the naturalist station learning about the different plants native to the rainforest. This topic is so ripe for building that intelligence!"

Mr. Corby continues excitedly, "These are going to be such well-rounded students! I can't wait to make more lessons into learning stations! I have great ideas for upcoming lessons in mathematics, social science, and language arts. I think this can be a great avenue for rigorous learning activities that equip students with skills to be successful academically and even later professionally."

Mrs. Hamilton hesitates before responding, "OK, I agree, for the most part you are right and it is going well. Although, I don't know if you visited some of the groups I observed . . . but, it isn't all 'fun and games,' some students are actually struggling when trying to complete these activities. While we expected some would need more of our assistance, some are needing a great deal of guidance. So we might want to make a note as we move forward as to the most effective ways to organize activities that successively build on students' understanding with increasing levels of difficulty as students grasp the level below."

Mrs. Hamilton continues, "Perhaps rather than letting students choose, we consider organizing small groups around students' mastery level? And I think I saw some students struggling with the more independent learning skills that these centers depend on. But, don't get me wrong . . . I think we are onto something here. We just have to find the ideal way to use this method most effectively."

As the teachers talk, Mr. Corby has kept his eyes on the class and notices another group of students clapping their hands in wonderment of a learning breakthrough. He excuses himself to rush over and congratulate them on their progress. At the same time, Mrs. Hamilton notices the problem between Lance and Avery is beginning to escalate once more. The boys are yelling at each other, and she fears a physical altercation is soon to follow. Unfortunately, it doesn't seem that these two boys will be able to successfully work together.

While she makes her way back to the pair, she makes a mental note to return to the issues she and Mr. Corby had begun to discuss. Clearly there are challenges to teaching through these learning centers that she doesn't think either teacher fully anticipated, and they will need to revisit them. But then again, she couldn't deny the rewards. However, she wonders how much of the curriculum should really be taught in such a fashion?

DISCUSSION QUESTIONS

1. Gardner's Theory of Multiple Intelligences:

   a. Identify the types of intelligence do you see evidence of in this case.
   b. Invent other ways these teachers might have conducted the lessons using Howard Gardner's theory of multiple intelligences?
   c. Point out myths or inappropriate uses of Gardner's theory. For instance, distinguish between Gardner's types of intelligence and that of learning styles.
   d. Do you think these teachers have adopted a realistic and appropriate use of Gardner's theory into the classroom? Discuss the myth that teachers should try to teach through each of the eight types of intelligence.

e. Can you evaluate your own intelligence profile according to Gardner? In what frames of mind do you rate the strongest?

2. Goleman's Emotional Intelligence (EQ):

   a. What are symptoms of low emotional intelligence? Specifically, describe the role of managing emotions and recognizing the emotions of others.
   b. Do you agree with the proposition that EQ is a better predictor for an individual's success in life than more standard definitions of intelligence?
   c. Describe the nature of emotional intelligence in the interchange between Avery and Lance.
   d. How might the teachers have bolstered students' abilities in emotional intelligence to optimize learning situations? How can educators help students manage emotions proactively? How might stories be used as a platform to discuss empathy, personal responsibility, communication, and conflict resolution skills.
   e. Compare and contrast the concept of emotional intelligence with elements of Gardner's and Sternberg's theories.

3. Sternberg's Theory of Successful Intelligence:

   a. What are the elements to Sternberg's successful theory of intelligence?
   b. Which types of intelligence do you see evidence of in this case?
   c. Ascertain how students scoring lower on traditional testing might perform more strongly in other types of intelligence.
   d. Contrast this view of intelligence from that of Gardner.
   e. Discuss how an understanding of this view of intelligence aids classroom teachers' decision making.

4. Planning for Constructivist Learning:

   a. What are important lesson planning strategies for utilizing learning centers most effectively in the classroom?
   b. Describe an authentic, problem-based learning activity that could be used as an alternative to learning centers the teacher might consider for the unit on threats to the rainforest, environmental impact, and potential environmental solutions.
   c. What classroom management considerations should be taken into account when designing learning centers?
   d. What assessment considerations should be taken into account when planning for learning centers?
   e. Offer other examples of modifications that can be infused to regular instruction to account for students with differing levels of mastery. In

particular, discuss impact of individualized instruction or differentiated instruction.

5. Socioemotional Development:

   a. Discuss the connection between the research literature on emotional intelligence and that of socioemotional development.
   b. What is the role of teachers in encouraging students' social-emotional understanding? How can teachers help children develop understanding of people's behavior, feelings, thoughts, and individual characteristics?
   c. How might teachers help students develop positive relationships with their peers? How might literature and discussion help students handle the social problems typical to elementary school?

Case 7

Teaching Diverse Learners

Connecting Home and School Cultures

Suggested Theories/Content: Diversity, Multicultural Education, and Bilingualism
Teacher Challenges: Poverty, SES, and Technology
Student Level: Upper Elementary School

Luciana and Valeria are twin sisters whose family are local migrant workers. They are both fifth-graders at La Costa Valley Elementary School, and their school has a Spanish-speaking student demographic that is higher than in other districts in the state. The majority of the kids in their class are bilingual whose first language is Spanish. Their teacher, Jayson Moore, is new this year to their school, but thus far the students really like him. "Hi Luciana!" Ignacio says as he and his neighbor Rodrigo walk up to the school from where buses disembark and meet up with Luciana and her sister who are arriving from the other direction since they walk to school.

"Hi Ignacio! Hi Rodrigo!" Luciana responds in a friendly manner. "What did you think of the vocabulary homework last night? It took forever, right?" Ignacio asks shaking his head, Rodrigo adds annoyed, "Yeah it did, I couldn't play on my Xbox because it took so long to finish it, and then I had to study for the test today. But without that practice the tests are too hard." Valeria shakes her head and says, "Well, no wonder Luciana and I aren't doing too good! We never get to those extra activities because we have no internet at home or a computer."

Ignacio smiles sympathetically and says, "I know. . . . I don't either, but luckily our neighbor watches all my brothers and me and she lets us use her computer." Rodrigo nods his head with understanding and says, "Too bad we all don't live near each other because you all could come over and use mine." They all agree that would be great, but Rodrigo's house is not within walking distance to the school or to the other students' houses, and there is no one home to drive any of them after school. "Have you all told Mr. Moore that you can't do all those other things because you don't own a tablet or computer? He's so nice, maybe he could help," Rodrigo says.

Their teacher Mr. Moore is standing in the doorway of their classroom happily welcoming the students in. "Hey there, good morning!" Mr. Moore says to Luciana, Valeria, Rodrigo, and Ignacio, and they all greet him in return and enter the classroom and take their seats. Mr. Moore notices that the twins Luciana and Valeria are once again dressed in clothes that appear too large for them, and he knows that their family regularly takes advantage of the donated uniforms the office receives at the beginning of the school year.

He hopes the girls have brought their signed paperwork to qualify them for the reduced or free snack and lunch that the front office staff said they needed to have on file. He makes a note to ask them later privately as to not cause embarrassment for the girls in front of the other classmates. As the last students take their seats, Mr. Moore is ready to begin the day. He begins by outlining the changes to their reading unit that will allow for a technology component to be added. Mr. Moore has been revising his curriculum out of concern for the grades of some of his ESOL (English for Speakers of Other Languages) students.

He has always used instructional materials that include examples and contexts relevant to students' cultures, so that they have a familiar foundation and can relate their school work to their home culture. Recently, he has also added a technology component to his instructional strategies because he has learned that using technology will allow for individualized pacing, visual organizers, and opportunities to emphasize key vocabulary words—all factors that assist his ESOL students' learning.

Mr. Moore knows that all students easily become engaged with the media-rich environment provided by educational software and educational websites, and he sees technology as fun and exciting for all students and thereby an effective strategy for enhancing all students' learning. "So class, I think you are going to like this new change to our reading unit. I am allowing all of you to use the computers here at school for the activities that go along with the unit which will let you click on words you don't understand for definitions and give you extra practice if you need it."

Mr. Moore smiles as he looks around the room and continues, "I am assigning you to work in teams so that if one of you is having trouble, the other can help out! I plan on having time set aside in class each day that will allow for all of the teams to have a chance to work on the computers." There seems to be a mixed reaction on the part of the students. "Yes, Alonso do you have a question?" Mr. Moore asks since Alonso's hand is up. "What if we don't finish doing the work on the reading unit in class? Can we take what we don't finish home? But then how do we work with our partners?" Alonso asks.

"Well," says Mr. Moore thoughtfully considering the question, "sure you can finish at home, and you can work together via phone, texting, or you can always use the instant messaging feature that is offered on the reading textbook's site. Your username and password for the textbook's site are listed on each of your reading unit folders that you will be taking with you to the computer stations when working. A reminder if you are going to use your parent's phones, tablets, iPad, etc. please be sure to get their permission!" Students laugh and now the mood seems to be lighter.

Mr. Moore starts assigning the first three teams to go to the computers and reminds them to use their time wisely since there are only six computers in the classroom for them all to share. Luciana and Bobby are one of the teams working on the computer, "Bobby I am still not sure I understand what this question is trying to get us to do? Can you go back and highlight the area that we are supposed to read again?" Luciana asks and Bobby agrees. Soon however, their time on the computer comes to an end, and Luciana sees that they have only completed a third of the work while other teams have completed much more.

"Luciana, we are gonna have to talk tonight to finish this. Here is my contact information and my mom's. Call or text to either one so we can talk," Bobby says as he hands Luciana the piece of paper where he has written down the phone numbers. "Hmm, well, I'll see what I can do Bobby because I don't have a cell phone," Luciana says nervously. "Oh yeah, many kids don't, but just use your mom or dad's, or if use your tablet and are on Wi-Fi, you can text me," replies Bobby.

"Well, hum, I don't have a tablet," Luciana stammers in a whisper but Bobby has already walked away believing that they'll talk tonight. Luciana walks by her sister's desk and sees her sister's reading unit is also unfinished. "Valeria, you all didn't get far either huh? How are we going to get this work done without a computer at home?" Luciana asks pointing at their papers and continues, "or a cell phone or iPad to talk to the other kids, ugh, I think we need to talk to Mr. Moore . . . see if he can give us more time or I don't know . . . help us I guess."

Valeria sighs and says "I know and well we can't stay after school to use the computers here because mom said that only kids in aftercare can do that, and she can't pay for aftercare. And remember when we tried walking to the library, the lady there said we needed an adult with us. . . . Grandma can't walk that far anymore." Luciana sadly nods her head in agreement.

The class is taking out their snacks and students are joining various friend groups to enjoy the social time that snack time affords them. Mr. Moore's policy is that the kids can sit with friends as long as they do not get too loud. If they do, they have to return to their seats and eat their snack alone. Luciana and Valeria walk over to the group of kids that are congregating by the door as Mr. Moore says "OK gang, all of you forgot snacks today I see. Alright walk together to the lunchroom to get the free snack and you know the drill— please come quickly back."

Upon the students return, Mr. Moore seizes this opportunity to ask the girls about the paperwork the office needs for their snack/lunch help. They tell him that they do not have it with them because their mom didn't finish filling it out. Apparently their mom had to leave town to care for a sick relative and left them in care of their grandmother who doesn't speak English and can't fill out the forms. "How about the field-trip forms? Was your mom able to sign those before she left?" Mr. Moore asks. Both girls shake their head and look down at their feet.

"You know ladies that if I don't have the signed field-trip forms by the end of the week, you won't be able to go," Mr. Moore says kindly before adding, "I have tried repeatedly to contact your mom both via phone and sent her several email messages but have received no reply. Do you know how else I can contact her?" Luciana doesn't answer. Valeria, after a pause, answers in a quiet voice, "No . . . not really. She has a cell phone but the number changes because they are the ones you throw away. . . . I don't know about her email. We talk to her at night when she calls us. I will tell her to call you." Mr. Moore smiles and says, "Great, thank you!"

After snack time, the class moves into their cooperative learning groups. They are working on a jigsaw cooperative learning exercise in social studies where each group member is working in their "expert meetings" on a portion of the assignment that was selected from the teacher-prepared materials. They have returned to their original heterogenous groups, in terms of ethnicity and gender, to share their findings when Mr. Moore notices one group is experiencing some trouble they are not likely to resolve without intervention.

"Seriously Rodrigo, we can't say in our final paper that being a farmer is a good idea! Farmers don't make any money! Why would anyone want to be a farmer?" Ryan asks with a sigh. "Well farming was an occupation that gave people a lot of money back then. . . . I didn't say it is a good idea now!" Rodrigo says clearly irritated. As Mr. Moore talks with the group about being able to communicate to each other respectfully, he doesn't miss the hurt expression on Catalina's face.

It is clear that Catalina has obviously taken the comment to heart given her migrant family background and the fact that this was her idea for her group to explore. Mr. Moore ensures that the students apologize to Catalina for not respecting her feelings. He makes a point to later conclude the large-group discussion with the importance of valuing the merits of diverse occupations and how each has a role to fulfill in society.

Unfortunately, Mr. Moore doesn't get very far circling among the cooperative learning groups before one of the students at the computer stations demands his attention. "Mr. Moore, Grayson is not giving me enough time on the computer," Ignacio says. Grayson quickly adds, "That's not true! I'm actually doing all of the work! Ignacio is going to the wrong websites, and he takes forever opening up other tabs so we can go back and forth getting information from more than one place at a time! And he types really slow. . . . We'll never get this done if I let him use the computer, and you said computer time is limited!"

Mr. Moore can see by accessing the boys' history on the computer that Ignacio is not trying to be off-task by purposely going to the wrong websites, but that the websites are misspelled, and he has seen that Ignacio is a slower typer. All of this points to Ignacio's lack of technological expertise due to his lack of experience with technology, not because he is lacking the ability.

His hunch is confirmed when Ignacio indeed reveals that he has never owned a tablet or computer, and that he only gets to use his neighbor's computer when she is watching them after school. But his older brothers get to use it first since they have more to do. Mr. Moore gets the boys back on track working together and heads to the back of the room where one of his ESOL students is working with his assigned buddy.

The two students are seated in the back of the classroom working on a reading activity. The ESOL student, Miguel Alejandro, is in the process of asking his reading buddy, Brenda, what the author means by a portion of the text. Mr. Moore smiles as he watches Brenda and Miguel work together by clicking on the link that will provide clarification, and then Brenda begins to share her own experiences with the circus which is the subject of the reading passage. Her sharing of personal experiences is helping shed light on the difficult reading passage for Miguel Alejandro by giving him visuals and more details than the story provides.

The reading buddy system is one of the ESOL reading strategies Mr. Moore added to his instruction as his number of ESOL students increased. This is primarily because the reading passages contain references to various cultures and hence can be matched to the student's home culture. He has also infused small-group discussions to allow ESOL students to practice their verbal skills, has set up learning centers that offer additional and alternative instruction that reinforces the lessons, and has equipped those learning centers with bilingual dictionaries.

ESOL students also come to him at the end of the day if they need better directions on homework assignments, since the ESOL students lack the English language support at home. The ESOL coordinator for the school shared with him the other day that the ESOL students are not only enjoying the new instructional strategies he is implementing, but they are benefiting from them.

During the last hour of the day, Mr. Moore has promised his students that as a special treat for working diligently all week he is going to let them work on their art work for the school-wide contest. The students are all very excited to enter the art contest, because the art teacher will choose the top five best drawings and award each of them a prize. Mr. Moore sees that many of this students will be entering very creative works of art that vary in the materials used to depict the scene they are portraying.

However, he sighs as he notices many students are still sharing supplies with others because they have yet to bring in their own even though it's been more than two months since the school year began. Luciana and Valeria are among the students lacking their colored pencils, markers, crayons, etc. In fact, with the exception of a few pencils and a few pens that the girls share, he hasn't seen any other supplies in their desks and neither one of them owns a pencil case.

Other students seated near the girls are always very gracious in sharing their supplies; however, he knows that several parents have complained to him that they feel that their child's supplies seem to be getting used up faster than should be expected, and that they do not want to continuously be buying supplies when other students do not bring any in. Mr. Moore makes a note to ask the administration what can be done to assist the students without supplies.

It is the end of the week and Mr. Moore sits at his desk pondering the response rate to invitations his class sent to their parents inviting them to the class presentations on the social studies unit. Nita Pellegrini, who teaches down the hall, walks by his class and pokes her head in and says good-naturedly "hard at work as usual, huh, Jayson? Always raising the bar for the rest of us I see." Jayson smiles sheepishly and replies, "Not so much trying to raise the bar as attempting to stay one step ahead of my students! Never let them see you sweat, right?"

Nita laughs and agrees before saying "I heard you are doing presentations where the students invited their parents; are you getting a good turn out?" Jayson and Nita talk about the nature of the student presentations, and Jayson shares his concern in the lack of parent response. "In fact, not only have many parents turned down the invitation to come to the presentations, but there's a very low number of parent chaperones for the field trip next week. I get the distinct impression there are more than work schedules and commitments getting in the way of their participating in the classroom. Do you get that feeling as well with the parents of your students?"

Nita takes a seat in a chair across from Jayson's desk before replying. "Yes, I do. In fact, I don't think that many parents purposely choose to not get involved, but rather they may truly be unable to get involved because taking time off work may not be possible for them. Remember that many of our students come from diverse backgrounds and cultures, and that some families from different cultural backgrounds may not feel confident coming into the school and participating or may think it isn't their place to get involved. I think it is unfair when some teachers automatically assume that our students' parents don't want to be involved."

Jayson thinks reflectively to conversations he has had with his students that have shed light into their home cultures, and he remembers that many are being taken care of by relatives who lack formal schooling having given up school in favor of helping their families. Other caregivers lack transportation and/or do not speak English and rely on the child to be their translator.

Taking Jayson's silence as agreement, Nita asks, "You have Ignacio in your class right?" Jayson nods and Nita continues, "I have one of his younger brothers in my class this year and had his sister in my class last year. They come from a large migrant family with kids ranging from a few months old to high school, and it is my understanding that their neighbor, as well as other family members, take turns watching the children so their parents do not lose valuable work time. Whenever I had to meet with them to discuss one of their children's progress they either had to rely on public transportation or borrow a vehicle since they do not have one of their own."

Nita pauses before continuing, "however, they were always very interested in their children's education, and I could tell they were doing all they could to ensure their kids stayed on track. The same is true with the families of the African American students I had in my class over the years. Actually Jayson, you ought to try finding some way for parents of diverse cultures to be involved in helping their children in the home environment."

Jayson sighs and runs his hand through his hair thinking about the Chinese-American student in his class. His parents are very active in helping him with school work at home, but they were among the group that has not responded to the school-based classroom volunteer opportunities. Jayson then says, "I completely agree with you, I don't think I was considering all of the different factors present here, in particular, to being sensitive to parents of other cultures and how different cultures might view their roles in their children's education. I have to be honest I have never felt very confident about my own abilities to reach parents."

Jayson, clearly exasperated continues, "sure, we all had some exposure to parental involvement in our teacher preparation programs, but I guess I am just not up-to-date! I guess I have a bit of homework myself!" Nita laughs at the last bit and offers to give Jayson some of the resources that she uses and share some tips that she has found have worked over the years creating effective bridges between the home and school cultures.

DISCUSSION QUESTIONS

1. Multicultural Education:

   a. What is multicultural education? How can teaching be more "culturally relevant"?

   b. What is the relationship between SES (socioeconomic status) and achievement? In what ways are children from impoverished backgrounds likely to have difficulty in school?

    c. In what ways has the use of the Jigsaw cooperative learning model been shown to be advantageous in creating culturally compatible classrooms? What are other ways teachers can improve relationships among children from different ethnic groups?

    d. What learning styles/preferences have been uncovered that might apply to the Hispanic students in Mr. Moore's class? Applying this information, how effective do you think this teacher's instruction will be with ESOL students? What could be some negative effects of applying the same learning styles to all cultural groups uniformly?

    e. Compare and contrast how your own experiences with people of diverse ethnic groups have been similar to or different from what you have heard or previously believed about those groups.

    f. How would you evaluate Mr. Moore's responsiveness to cultural diversity? Has his conversation with the other teacher helped to expand his views? What suggestions would you make?

2. Bilingualism:

    a. Evaluate the teacher's effectiveness with his bilingual students. Is the teacher receptive to changes in his instruction? Are the changes in his instruction made with bilingual students in mind?

    b. Multimedia and other technologies are enhancing opportunities for bilingual students and LEP (Limited English Proficient) students. Evaluate the ways in which the teacher in this case is using such technologies in his classroom. Are there other technologies that you have studied that can assist ESOL and LEP students?

    c. Construct some strategies for scaffolding of reading concepts for students as they master the English language.

    d. Synthesizing across the literature on effective teaching for students in bilingual and ESOL classrooms, what strategies do you think would be effective in Mr. Moore's class?

3. Parent Involvement:

    a. Identify the range of types of parent involvement the teacher in this case might become familiar with as he attempts to encourage involvement in his classroom.

    b. Extending on the two teachers' conversation at the end of the case with regard to parent involvement, how may a teacher engage parents who do not feel it is their place to be involved in the classroom?

    c. Other than conflicts with their job, outline possible reasons parents may have for not becoming involved. How can a teacher assist parents to feel more empowered about becoming involved in the classroom?

d. Analyze how having students that have different home cultures from their school culture create conflicts in teachers' attempts at parent involvement. What are possible strategies that can help in bridging that gap?

e. What resources and helpful tips could a teacher give to parents in order to communicate the importance that parent involvement has for their child's academic success?

f. How can the use of technology and the internet be beneficial in overcoming obstacles in handling hard-to-reach parents?

g. Discuss creative and innovative ideas for overcoming common obstacles parents might experience in coming to the class so they may remain involved in their children's education?

4. Educational Technology:

a. In this case, the teacher uses technology in the classroom to enhance his reading and social studies instruction. What other ways can technology be used in the classroom across all subject areas to increase the effectiveness of instruction?

b. How can teachers use educational software, tablets, iPad, and computers to enhance student's educational experiences? What are the pros and cons of bringing these technological tools into the classroom?

c. In this case the teacher is faced with students who are living in poverty. How can the use of technology widen the learning gap between the more affluent students and the disadvantaged ones?

d. Discuss how the use of technology might widen the learning gap between different ethnic backgrounds. What are the recommendations for reducing inequity with regard to computer use?

e. What precautions should teachers take when bringing technology into their classrooms? What obstacles and potential pitfalls can they face with regard to children and the internet?

f. How can a teacher's own technology beliefs and effectiveness affect the degree to which they use technology in their classrooms? How can schools help to increase teachers' technological skills so that they may feel more efficacious when using technology in their classrooms and helping their students?

Case 8

Gender Stereotypes

A Look into the Early Childhood Classroom

Suggested Theories/Content: Gender Roles, Gender Differences, Socialization of Gender Roles, and Early Childhood Behaviors in relation to Gender Social Development

Teacher Challenges: Sexism and Gender Stereotypes, Equitable Teaching Practices

Student Level: Kindergarten

"Cameron! Switch with me. I don't want to color the grasshopper, I want to color the ladybug!" Mia exclaims, exasperated. "Okay Mia, here," Cameron says resignedly as he switches activity projects with his classmate. "Yay!" Mia claps her hands happily, holding the prized ladybug paper. The teacher, Ms. Giuliana, walks over to the table of her kindergarten students and says, "Mia, you cannot keep asking other students to switch with you when you are given a task or project to do that you do not like."

Ms. Giuliana squats next to Mia and continues, "Yesterday you switched computer stations with Martino during math time because you wanted to work on the computer game that had flowers instead of the one you were assigned to, which was construction. You also did this last week when we played spelling games on the iPad—wanting only the game that was princess dress-up. Remember? We talked about this, Mia. The game or the picture is not what is important because the purpose of the game is to practice the lessons you are learning."

Mia stops coloring and says in a whiny tone, "I know . . . but . . . but, Ms. Giuliana, I did not wanna play on the construction game—it had trucks, and you had to push the different piles of dirt together to get the right answer! It was yucky boy stuff!" "Mia, while I understand you may not always like what I assign, you have to do it. This is your last warning. Is that understood?"

Ms. Giuliana asks Mia, her tone a bit sterner now than when she began speaking with her. Mia is clearly upset but she nods her head in response. Ms. Giuliana smiles at her but isn't fully convinced that Mia will stop trying to get her way.

"Okay class," Ms. Giuliana claps her hands to gain the students' attention and directs them to their next activity. "Please put your completed work in your cubby and let's get ready for centers. Remember that the center that you are at each day is listed on the green board, so look for your name and go to your assigned center." As the students begin their center work, Ms. Giuliana circulates among them to ensure they are on-task and discovers that Cameron is not in his center. "Cameron, where are you supposed to be?" Ms. Giuliana asks.

"I dunno," Cameron says as he looks down at his shoe. "Well, let's go look at the green board together and see what center you belong at," Ms. Giuliana says as she motions for Cameron to follow her to the green board. Together they discover that Cameron should be in the cooking center, not the building center where he was. Ms. Giuliana sees the reluctance in Cameron as she walks with him to where the cooking center is located. "Something wrong Cameron?" Ms. Giuliana asks.

"I don't like the cooking center, cooking is for girls. I don't want to go there. I want to stay in the building center—that is for boys . . . my daddy says so," Cameron says sullenly. Ms. Giuliana talks calmly to him about all the virtues of cooking and shares many of the names of the famous chefs around the world who are men. "In my house," Ms. Giuliana adds, "my husband does all the cooking. He is really good at it! His food is delicious!" Cameron smiles although he still looks a bit skeptical, and Ms. Giuliana walks away to assist students in another center.

Amber, who is at the cooking center, says to Cameron, "Boy are you lucky! She didn't yell at you or nothing for trying to get out of being here." Cameron looks surprised and asks, "What do you mean Amber?" "Well," Amber says lowering her voice to a whisper before continuing, "when Mia switched her paper with you earlier Ms. Giuliana got mad and reprimanded her, but you have done the same thing before too—and now you purposely went to the wrong center and you didn't get yelled at or nothing." Cameron smiles broadly and says, "Guess she likes me more then." Amber as well as the other students in the center all nod in agreement.

During recess, two students come to Ms. Giuliana to ask her to help them resolve a dispute. Winston is upset that he is not being allowed to play the animal that he wants in the pretend game they invented. "Ms. Giuliana, I want to be the pink princess giraffe in the game, but Amber says I can't be because all the pink princess giraffes are the girls. If I want to play, I can only be a blue lion," Winston says as the tears begin to fall down his face. Ms. Giuliana places her hand on Winston's shoulder and says kindly, "Winston, do not cry. It is only a game and remember, people always say that boys don't cry."

Ms. Giuliana turns to Amber and asks firmly, "Please explain to me why you aren't letting Winston play the game?" Amber looks troubled but answers, "Ms. Giuliana, the pink princess giraffes are girls! Only girls are princesses and they like pink! Winston is a boy and that is why we told him to be the blue lion!" Amber pauses for a moment and continues, exasperated, "It's just like my shoes, they are girl shoes—but Winston wants a pair just like them!" Mia, who is standing next to Amber, quickly adds, "Yes! Ms. Giuliana, they're girl shoes with princesses, crowns, and jewels that light up! Boys aren't princesses or pink princess giraffes! Everyone knows that!"

"See, look!" Mia finishes with emphasis as she points at both her and Amber's colorful shoes and both girls jump in place to demonstrate the lights flashing from the jewels. "Yes, I see the lights; however, you all have hurt your classmate's feelings. If you can't include all students who want to play, then I'm not allowing any of you to play it anymore. So work it out," Ms. Giuliana says evenly, but decisively, to what is now a large group of her female students who have wandered over to hear the resolution to the game dilemma. The students all walk away since Ms. Giuliana doesn't hear any more on the subject. She assumes they have resolved their differences.

Ms. Giuliana looks up to see the school's coach, Coach Zack, momentarily stopped on the other side of the playground fence where he is putting away some of the physical education equipment. "Hey there! Couldn't help but overhear your playground dilemma over the colored animals, seems like you are used to handling those situations by how quickly you resolved it!" Coach Zack says good-naturedly.

"Oh yes, it is all part of a kindergarten teacher's territory!" Ms. Giuliana says with a quiet laughter before continuing, "Unfortunately that will not be the end of the disagreements. You know how there are students who will always get upset if they do not get their way. Yesterday our new math journals arrived and the students were all excited, as they have been looking forward to this unit. This was, of course, until they saw the covers for the journals, which depicted a female caterpillar as a mathematician. Immediately, several boys expressed their displeasure!"

Ms. Giuliana shakes her head and continues, "They told me everyone knew that boys are the ones that are good at math, not girls—so it should have been a boy caterpillar on the cover. Soon, they all wanted to voice their opinions and the entire classroom was in chaos. I guess it's all part of this age group!"

Coach Zack laughs and says, "I sympathize with you but you know I face these issues all the time in physical education as well, but I find it pertains to all the ages and depends more on the individual child."

Coach Zach continues, "Some girls do not want to partake in certain sports because they think of it as a boy sport, and the same is true for boys with sports they view as being more feminine. I have found that their parents also share that mindset. For the upcoming field day, I had several parents talk to me regarding the games—I have a couple of fathers complain to me that their sons should not have to jump rope because that is for girls."

As Ms. Giuliana listens, Coach Zach continues, "I explained how these events in the field day such as the three-legged race, the balloon toss, etc., are not gender-based and are fun for everyone. We want to have children recognize the importance of exercising and staying fit. I am not sure they were truly happy with my explanations, but at least they are letting their kids participate." Ms. Giuliana looks surprised at the coach's revelations. After all, she'd always assumed her students were having these problems because they wanted to impose their wills.

As the school day comes to a close, Ms. Giuliana engages in her Friday ritual of rotating the students' assigned classroom chores. She always makes sure to go over the chores together as a class, so that students are clear as to what their assigned chore are. Ms. Giuliana goes over to the chores board and begins assigning different chores to various students. "Ms. Giuliana, when will it be my turn to be a recess helper?" asks Gabby after raising her hand to speak and getting the teacher's permission.

"Gabby, we are getting ready to review our class chores for the new week's assignment, so we'll see what you are assigned," Ms. Giuliana replies before resuming, "Now, let's review our chores. Okay ladies, you have a choice between being a *class sweeper*, who will sweep the floor at the end of the day; a *whiteboard cleaner*, who will clean the whiteboards after they are used; a *display helper,* who will help me design and decorate the activity boards*; front office messenger*, who will take the attendance, as well as other communication, to the office; or a *paper handler* who passes out and collects papers, agendas, and homework."

"Gentlemen," Ms. Giuliana continues, "you will have a choice between a *recess helper*, who collects all playground equipment and runs it over to Coach Zack; a *media helper*, who will be in charge of turning media equipment off and on and adjusts volume; a *recycling chief*, who guarantees recycle bins are emptied frequently; *scrap paper collector*, who crawls around the floor and collects all scraps of paper after activities; or *door holder*, who holds the door for the entire class." The students are enthusiastic about their chores; Ms. Giuliana overhears a few girls commenting how happy they were not to be doing chores that will get them dirty. Ms. Giuliana is happy to hear this. Perhaps, she thinks to herself, she may face less problems come Monday then.

The following week, the students are finishing with their career presentations. It is part of a month-long unit the class has been involved in where they have been learning about the jobs in their community. Her students have taken field trips to local establishments to learn about jobs and careers first-hand and have had community members come to the school to talk about their jobs. It all led to the final part of the unit where the students have chosen an occupation to study and make a brief presentation to the class.

Today is the last day of the presentations and thus far Ms. Giuliana has been very pleased with the students' work. All of her students have done a wonderful job with some students bringing props, drawings, collages, and pictures to help explain the job they chose. "Alright class, let's all give our attention to Gabby who is up next!" Ms. Giuliana says from her desk as Gabby walks up with a giant model airplane and puts on a pilot's cap, clearly indicating that Gabby's career is airline pilot.

Next it is Winston's turn, and he has chosen to discuss as his occupation. He brought a large poster board with pictures and a play medical kit as he talks about what nurses do. Finally, it is the last student's turn to present and, since the students are presenting in alphabetical order, it is Cameron's turn since his last name begins with a W. Cameron presents on his chosen career—architect and uses a model of a building made out of building blocks as a prop. Ms. Giuliana is pleased to see all her students' creativity on display as they presented on their careers.

As the students line up to go to lunch, Ms. Giuliana overhears many of them offering negative comments on both Gabby's and Winston's choice of occupations. Many students tell Gabby that being an airline pilot is for men and tell Winston that being a nurse is a woman's job. Gabby defends her choice telling them that she likes planes and hopes to fly one when she is older and shares that her room is decorated with cars and planes. Rather than putting an end to the quarrel, Gabby's admission seems to have made it worse, as now many of the kids are telling her that girls don't decorate their rooms with cars and planes.

Ms. Giuliana puts a stop to the arguing and has the students teasing Gabby issue apologies while she tries to help Gabby stop crying. Ms. Giuliana definitely wasn't expecting this bickering to ensue and is, in fact, taken aback to hear her students expressing dislike over other students' career choices. She thought she did a good job demonstrating to her students that there are a vast number of career choices.

Ms. Giuliana made sure that even when it came to the students' parents who came to present on their occupations that there were an even number of mothers and fathers. There were three fathers and three mothers: Amber's father who is a doctor, Nathan's father who is a mechanic, Hank's father who is a firefighter, Cameron's mother who is a hairdresser, Anita's mother who is a secretary, and Ruth's mother who is a dental assistant.

The following day, Ms. Giuliana is on the reading carpet as her students gather around her listening to their afternoon story. The students know that after they listen to their story they will need to go back to their desks and work on their timeline puzzle of the story they just heard. "Okay class, are there any questions before you go back to work on the activity?" Ms. Giuliana asks and signals for Mia to speak.

"How come none of the animals that were the bravest in the story were girls?" Mia asks. Ms. Giuliana reflects back to the story she just read the class and says in earnest, "Hmm, I don't know Mia. That is a good question." "I know! I know!" shouts Hank, without raising his hand before speaking, and continues proudly, "My big brother says it's because boys are brave fighters who protect everyone and aren't afraid of anything!" Ms. Giuliana smiles at Hank and asks if there are any other questions before sending all the students back to their desks.

Ms. Giuliana soon hears students arguing. "I like this pencil case, its dinosaurs. It's not just for boys, my mommy said I could have it 'cause it matches my backpack. And I'm not a boy! I'm a girl," Anita says angrily at Hank. "Anita has a boy pencil case, Anita is a boy!" Hank says in a singing voice. Ms. Giuliana turns to Hank and asks, "Now Hank, what have I said about being mean to classmates?" Hank immediately looks contrite and says, "That we shouldn't be, but, um, I was just playing around with Anita. . . . I didn't mean to hurt her feelings. Honest!"

Ms. Giuliana decides this is a perfect opportunity to talk to the class about a change in her classroom policies. "Class, since we all seem to be having trouble getting along and being nice to each other, I have decided to change to rules. You will now only receive one warning. If you continue to be unkind then you will lose half of your recess time. If I speak to you again that day, then you will lose all of your recess time the next day. I hope I am making myself very clear that hurting other's feelings will not be tolerated." There are many groans heard in the room, and Ms. Giuliana hopes that by toughening up her consequences her students' behavior will improve.

DISCUSSION QUESTIONS

1. Gender Differences and Stereotypes:

   a. How early are children taught information regarding gender? How do those early influences have the potential to shape a child's conception of gender?

   b. How are gender differences expressed socially in the classroom and how are the students' beliefs about gender affecting their relationships in this classroom?

   c. In this case, there are several students who seem to prefer certain colors, activities, etc. that are traditionally associated with the opposite gender while some are abiding strictly to what is gender-appropriate.

Explain how these students' choices and their classmate's reactions could affect their self-esteem and self-concept?

d. Discuss what a gender stereotype is and what gender stereotypes are evident in this case. What problems are created in this case as a result of students' gender stereotypes?

e. Discuss the meaning of a gender role. How do gender roles play a role in a child's understanding of jobs and careers? Were the gender roles expressed in this case displaying a bias toward a specific gender? Why or why not?

f. Examine how the career unit demonstrated gender roles. From the standpoint of gender, what possible problems were inherent in this unit that the teacher seemed to miss? Was it the teacher's intent to reinforce traditional gender roles? Why or why not?

2. Development and Socialization of Gender Roles:

a. Explain how a child forms gender schemas with regard to how males and females are different. Discuss how a child's environmental experiences with what is traditionally acceptable for each gender help to build their gender schemas and inform their behavior with regard to gender.

b. In the case, it is clear that some students are adhering to traditional gender stereotypes while others are not. Discuss examples of where these children may have learned their concept of gender and why some students are strictly abiding by those stereotypes.

c. What role does the "self-fulfilling" prophecy have in perpetuating gender roles and gender stereotypes? Do you see evidence that this could be a possible outcome in some of the students in this class? Why or why not?

d. Evaluate how parents can be a major factor in socializing gender role behavior. What evidence was presented in this case that would support this claim?

e. Assess how a parent, peer, teacher, or coach's behavior may unintendedly be accountable for imparting gender stereotypes. What evidence do you see of this in this classroom?

3. Equitable Teaching Practices:

a. Discuss how teachers can avoid sexism in their teaching. Ascertain what evidence of gender bias against either gender is evident in this case? Is the teacher aware that it is occurring? Discuss how gender bias can inadvertently occur in the classroom.

b. Assess how the teacher in this case is encountering gender stereotypes in her classroom. Is the teacher actively working to diminish the gender stereotypes that arise in her classroom? Alternatively, do you think this teacher is guilty of engaging in gender stereotypes herself? How could a teacher prevent their own gender stereotypes from coming across in the classroom?

c. Are there any instances of gender biases occurring with regard to the curriculum? Is the teacher aware that she is contributing to gender biases? What is the importance of acting in a way that diminishes rather than strengthening the gender biases in the classroom?

d. Judge how the teacher resolves disputes among her students that are clearly gender-based. Does the teacher handle those issues from a gender standpoint? Why or why not?

e. Discuss what the teacher's belief about gender seems to be and how it is being displayed in the case. Do you feel that the teacher's strategy of separating chores by gender is an appropriate and/or effective way to handle gender differences in the classroom? Why or why not?

f. At the end of the case the teacher opts for increasing classroom consequences for behavior in an effort to improve the social relations of her students. Judge this tactic's effectiveness in the absence of the teacher addressing the traditional gender roles and stereotypes that the students are exhibiting.

g. With the current trend for programs and careers in STEM (science, technology, engineering, and math) beginning at a young age, explain how a teacher not addressing traditional gender roles may prove a detriment for girls.

h. Research shows that gender inequality occurs for both females and males. Discuss the effects that these inequalities may pose for a young student's belief in their own ability, as well as how they see themselves in the future. In addition, how could it add to a self-fulfilling prophecy for both genders?

Part III

LEARNING THEORIES

Case 9

At What Cost?

Using Reinforcers
and Punishments in the Classroom

Suggested Theories: Applications of Operant Conditioning, Intermittent Reinforcement, Punishment, and Classroom Management, and Parent-Teacher Communication

Teacher Challenges: Reducing Negative Responses, Challenges of Using Rewards in the Classroom, and Communicating with Concerned Parents

Student Level: Lower Elementary

Mrs. Boyd is waiting in the conference room adjacent to her third-grade classroom for a student's parents to arrive for a parent-teacher conference. Mrs. Boyd had communicated with them a few times via emails and phone calls. However, she got the feeling that because they weren't getting the answers they wanted, they chose to call a conference. Once Harper's parents, Mr. and Mrs. Dunn, are seated across from her, they share their concerns. "We'd like you to explain what *Boyd Bucks* are, how the students earn them, and the goal that they work toward. Harper tells us she has very few while other children have many." Mrs. Dunn says.

"Well, I would have thought Harper would share this with you, but at any rate," Mrs. Boyd says and continues more enthusiastically after a short pause, "*Boyd Bucks* are tokens that students earn that can then be exchanged for *Reward Coupons*—four *Boyd Bucks* earn them one *Reward Coupon*. Students love the chance to choose a reward and redeem their *Reward Coupon* such as bringing a stuffed animal for the day, sitting in the teacher's chair for the day, getting to sit with a buddy for the day, being able to use sidewalk chalk at recess, or being able to choose a special pen from the teacher's desk and use it to write all day!"

"Similarly," Mrs. Boyd says, "we also have the *Lucky Hole-Punch Card* which is a small card that has designated spots for fifteen hole punches, and on it the student has chosen a goal that they want to work toward. Each *Hole-Punch* earned gets them closer to their goal. A student earns a hole punch at the end of each day if I feel that they have deserved it for being on-task all day!" Mr. and Mrs. Dunn nod their heads indicating their grasp on the behavior systems, and Mr. Dunn asks, "Do all students reach their goal? What happens when they reach their goal? Do they start over with a new goal?"

Mrs. Boyd shows much excitement as she answers, "Yes, they get to start over! All of my students have the potential to reach their goal! They love being able to choose a different goal! I give them choices like getting to select their class chore, moving freely around the room for a day without needing permission, or choosing the theme for the week's class mural and helping design it, and many more! I do not, however, keep track of which students have met their goals and which have not, that is something each student must do themselves. That is probably why I wasn't aware that Harper hasn't earned many *Boyd Bucks*."

Mrs. Boyd says reassuringly, "I give the students many chances to earn *Boyd Bucks* and *hole punches*; however, I am not surprised that Harper is falling behind because, for example, I give *Boyd Bucks* for homework, but her homework is often incomplete or incorrect. I also give *Boyd Bucks* for class participation, and while Harper raises her hand all the time to participate, she rarely gives the right answer." Mr. and Mrs. Dunn both look surprised as well as upset.

Mrs. Dunn speaks first, "Harper told us homework questions could be left blank if they didn't understand them because wrong answers didn't count against them. She said you told them homework was for practice. Students get the chance to fill in the answer the next day in class when you went over the work. So, if that is what she is doing, then why is her homework not worthy of *Boyd Bucks*? Also, are you certain the kids know exactly what meaningful participation is? Do they understand it means they have to answer the question correctly? Or do they think they just need to partake in the discussion? After all, they are very young."

Mrs. Boyd thinks on Mrs. Dunn's comments and then says, "Hmm, I don't recall having said that with regard to homework. All kids know what meaningful classroom participation is; I just think that Harper needs to work on paying closer attention." It is clear that Mr. and Mrs. Boyd are unhappy with their conversation, but then again she doesn't think many parents like being told their child is not doing well. Mr. Dunn asks a final question about the *Behavior Smiley Faces* and the negative consequences that the students face when they lose all their *Behavior Smiley Faces*.

"Well, once again, Harper really should be able to explain this to you because all the students know why they are being punished. The *Behavior Smiley Face* is a way for students to self-monitor their behavior, and it gives them chances to correct themselves before they get a punishment. Everyday students begin the day with three smiley faces attached with Velcro next to their names on the *Behavior Board*—the first happy face has a big smile, the second has a smaller smile, and the third has a worried smile.

When a student misbehaves, they remove the first smiley face; the second time they misbehave, they remove the second; and once a student has lost all their smiley faces, they are punished. Thus, the happy faces themselves are a visual representation of the student's own behavior status at all times." Mr. and Mrs. Dunn nod their understanding and Mrs. Dunn asks, "Are students able to go back and earn the smiley faces that they lost? What must they do? Because Harper says she tries, but you do not ever see her behaving and as a result she is punished."

Mrs. Boyd nods and says, "Yes, of course I let them earn back their smiley faces if they are engaging in the appropriate behaviors, but I'm afraid I rarely see Harper behaving after she's lost all her smiley faces and hence she often faces the negative consequence. You know, I wouldn't worry too much, Mr. and Mrs. Dunn. I have many years of teaching experience and it is likely Harper will improve as the year progresses." Mrs. Boyd finishes with the Dunns and walks back through the door that leads to her classroom; this way she can begin her preparation for her next lesson while her students are in art class.

Mrs. Boyd reflects on all the parent-teacher conferences she has had over the last few weeks which all reflect the same underlying theme—parents do not like their children being punished. Some parents, like the Dunns, wanted to dispute their children's lack of *Boyd Bucks*, others wanted to know why their children were being punished because, after all, they never got in trouble at home. Other parents had the nerve to tell her that she was too punitive, that they believed her methods were too advanced for third-graders to always follow, and that their children didn't always know what exactly she expected.

Additionally, some parents thought that her rewards systems like the *Lucky Hole-Punch Card* were unattainable to some students while easily reached by others who rapidly filled the *Lucky Hole-Punch Cards*. As a result, the kids believed she was playing favorites. Mrs. Boyd doesn't understand where all these problems could be coming from—after all she has been using many of these techniques for more than fifteen years and proved they work!

It's the end of the school day and students are being dismissed. A group of Mrs. Boyd's students are walking together toward the buses, "Did you fill your *Lucky Hole-Punch Card*?" Harper asks Levi in a gloomy tone. "Nah, did you?" Levi replies. Harper shakes her head no, but before she can continue, their classmate Antonella walks up and says cheerfully "Hey Harper! I got a *Reward Coupon* with my *Boyd Bucks* today, and I chose to sit next to a friend. Wanna sit next to me tomorrow?" Harper looks momentarily happy as she says, "Yeah! I'd love that!" Antonella looks from Levi to Harper and asks curiously, "What's up? You both look kinda sad."

Levi explains that he and Harper have never filled their *Lucky Hole-Punch Card* after weeks of trying, and they only have two *Boyd Bucks* each. It's likely that at this rate they'll never reach their goal or earn a *Reward Coupon*, even though other kids like Antonella have reached their goals multiple times. "Oh sorry, . . . I guess I didn't really notice because I've reached my goal a lot of times and got *Boyd Bucks*," Antonella replies caringly and adds, "Keep trying Okay? You all can do it." Though Harper doesn't look convinced, she and Levi both nod as they all board the bus together.

"Cool soccer keychain! Is that what you got with your *Boyd Bucks*?" Levi says to Isaac as his classmate sits next to him on the bus. "Yeah! I chose the treasure box; I was so glad it was still there! I saw it last week when I went to the treasure box after I had already picked the soccer pencils!" Levi rubs his fingers over the keychain and answers, "You're so lucky!" Antonella interrupts them since she and Harper are sitting behind Levi and Isaac and says, "Quit rubbing it in, Isaac . . . Levi and Harper didn't get a *Reward Coupon*." Isaac immediately looks apologetic. "No, don't worry about it you all, it's not your fault," Harper says.

"Wait, I just thought of something!" Antonella exclaims before resuming, "Why don't we ask my sister if she remembers more on Mrs. Boyd—maybe whatever she tells us can help you! She had her a couple of years ago. . . . you know my sister is super smart, so Mrs. Boyd loved her!" Antonella says excitedly and doesn't wait before waving her sister over as she enters the bus. Antonella's sister sits across the aisle from them, and soon she is sharing some information about Mrs. Boyd. "Renata, what was that you were telling me about trying to get Mrs. Boyd to sit you in the front or in the middle?" Antonella asks her sister quizzically.

"Oh yes, you know how Mrs. Boyd asks if you have trouble seeing the board or something like that? Well, ask for her to sit you in the first row, or if not then try to sit in the middle rows, never the outer rows or in the back because then she'll never see you being good. I mean I had to because I don't have great vision, but still if you ask her she'll do it. Because if not . . . you're not ever going to get hole punches or earn back the *Behavior Smiley Faces*," Renata says knowingly. Renata's friend nods her head and adds, "Yeah, remember that if Mrs. Boyd doesn't see you, then it did not happen in her book."

"Oh!" Renata exclaims and continues, "I know she says she doesn't care about wrong answers but she does—so if you don't know the answer, don't raise your hand to answer questions!" Harper looks ready to cry as she turns to Levi and says, "Looks like we've been doing it all wrong." Renata reaches over the seat and says kindly, "Hey! Hang in there! It'll get better. Lots of kids had trouble when I had her, and even their parents going and talking to her didn't really do much." Renata and Antonella say goodbye as the bus stop reaches their neighborhood stop.

The following day during science, a few students are goofing off while Mrs. Boyd works on getting her computer to start the slides for the lesson. Mrs. Boyd, clearly frustrated with the computer, is further troubled when she sees how many students are off-task. She calls out names for each student to remove one of their *Behavior Smiley Faces*. Isaac and Terrell immediately start to protest the removal of the *Behavior Smiley Face*, because they're on their last smiley faces which means they'll get a punishment. Mrs. Boyd ignores the boys' objections and asks them to spin the *Negative Consequence Wheel* to see what their punishment will be.

Even though Isaac is unhappy, he walks over to spin the *Negative Conse-quence Wheel*; his spin lands on *losing recess*. "Ah, no! That's when we all play soccer Mrs. Boyd," Isaac says dejectedly, but Mrs. Boyd ignores him and motions for Terrell to spin the *Negative Consequence Wheel*. Terrell complains the entire time he walks over to the wheel, worsening when his spin lands on *extra homework*. Still angry, Terrell kicks the leg of one of his classmate's desk as he walks back to his seat. "Terrell, now you have two punishments," Mrs. Boyd says firmly.

"What?!?" Terrell exclaims, outraged. "Yes," Mrs. Boyd says calmly, "you'll have extra homework and you'll stay with me for an hour after school before heading to aftercare. I'll call your parents to alert them to your punish-ment." Terrell tries to apologize in hope that Mrs. Boyd will remove one of the punishments, but Mrs. Boyd stays firm. As the science lesson continues, Mrs. Boyd has to send two more students to the *Negative Consequence Wheel* after losing all their smiley faces: Alexander, for talking disrespectfully to her, and Grace, for getting out of her seat without permission.

Alexander spins and gets *move desk next to the teacher*; he groans but walks back to his desk and starts dragging it to where Mrs. Boyd's desk is situated. Grace hesitantly walks up the large plastic wheel and spins. "Oh no! I have never seen this! I've landed on *take five marbles out of the class's jar!*" exclaims Grace anxiously, looking around the room as the disappointment registers on her classmates' faces. "But Mrs. Boyd, that is not fair, the class has worked so hard to have a movie day, and we are only one marble away! Please let me spin again."

Mrs. Boyd says as she assists Alexander in moving his desk next to hers, "No, Grace, you know there are no extra spins. You get what you spin. These punishments aren't unreasonable—even the new ones I just added. That is why it is so important to behave." Loud groans, moans, and sighs can be heard coming from the students as they express their displeasure at the sudden turn of events. Grace hangs her head as she removes the marbles from the class's jar and puts her head down as soon as she reaches her desk.

Later that week, Harper, Antonella, and DeShawn are sitting together working on their social studies project in the library. DeShawn has completed her *Lucky Hole-Punch Card* and reached her goal, and she chose *work at the library for half of the day*. Since Harper and Antonella are in her social studies group, they are joining her in the library. "So cool that you reached your goal again, DeShawn!" Antonella says and Harper nods in agreement.

"I was kinda in a rush because I was afraid Mrs. Boyd might take the hole punches away like she did the *Reading Rewards*. Remember?" DeShawn asks. "That was so unfair! I really liked getting all those rewards for reading books. Now that she got rid of the *Reading Rewards,* I'm not doing extra reading," Antonella answers. "Me neither. Why bother if you aren't gonna get rewards?" DeShawn asks, and they all giggle, but at seeing the librarian's frown they quickly get back to working quietly on their project.

DISCUSSION QUESTIONS

1. Applications of Operant Conditioning:

   a. Explain how Skinner's theory of Operant Condition plays a role in this case. How can this theory be effectively applied differently than it was applied in this case?

   b. Discuss the different positive reinforcers that this teacher is using in her classroom? Are they effectively modifying student behavior? Are they ones that are developmentally appropriate and engaging for this age group?

   c. Provide examples of how the teacher uses negative reinforcements in this class and if they are effective in increasing positive behaviors? What are the potential hazards of a teacher overusing reinforcers?

   d. Compare and contrast between the different intermittent schedules of reinforcement used in this case. Judge their effectiveness. Explain the schedule and the behavior the teacher is intending to reinforce by using this schedule.

   e. Conclude how they differ from continuous reinforcement and discuss when it would be most effective for a teacher to use continuous reinforcement and when it would be best to use intermittent reinforcement.

   f. The teacher in this case chooses to ignore some misbehaviors. Discuss what you believe her intention was with regard to the management of that behavior. Outline the ramifications a teacher should be aware of when ignoring students when they misbehave.

2. Motivation:

   a. Explain why you believe that some students are easily reaching their goals on the *Lucky Hole-Punch Card* or earning *Boyd Bucks* to trade in for *Reward Coupons* while others are not.
   b. At the end of the case the girls are discussing a removal of an existing *Reading Rewards*; discuss how the removal of that extrinsic reinforcer affected the students. How can using extrinsic reinforcers undermine the intrinsic value of a task for a student?
   c. Discuss the situation with Harper and Levi in this case and how their lack of attaining behavior goals and earning rewards may affect their self-concept and self-esteem. Identify instances from the case.
   d. What effect might repeated classroom failure have on a student's self-efficacy? Which student in this case might this relate to?
   e. Do you see evidence of mastery or performance orientation in the case?
   f. Identify how Harper and Levi's attributions may be affected by their lack of attaining behavior goals and earning the rewards that other classmates are attaining?
   g. The teacher in the case aims at using reinforcers to motivate students; however, how could students' intrinsic motivation be affected?

3. Punishment:

   a. Distinguish between the types of punishments that the teacher uses in this case. Are they proving effective in reducing students' behavior?
   b. The teacher uses both individual punishments and then introduces a group punishment that affects the entire class but that only one student earns—Taking marbles out of the class jar. Evaluate the effectiveness of such punishments.
   c. What are potential unintended side-effects of punishment in the classroom? Do you see evidence of any in the case? In particular, what effects does punishment have on a child's self-concept and self-esteem?
   d. What are some possible benefits of using negative reinforcement rather than using punishments?
   e. Outline the risks in overusing punishment and negative consequences with children.

4. Classroom Management:

   a. Identify this teacher's classroom management strategy, and discuss examples that support your answer.

b. Does this teacher's classroom represent an example of an organized and equitable environment for the students?

c. Evaluate *Boyd Bucks* as a token economy. Discuss their effectiveness on student behavior, as well as potential problems that are apparent in the case.

d. Discuss *Lucky Hole-Punch Card* as a token economy. Discuss their effectiveness on student behavior, as well as potential problems that are apparent in the case. Are the goals chosen for in these economy ones that students would work toward?

e. Deduce whether Mrs. Boyd demonstrates "withitness" in her classroom. What occurrences in this case speak to that?

f. The teacher in this case feels that the *Behavior Smiley Faces* provide students with self-monitoring. Taking into account the age of these students, do you believe this is successful for all students? Why or why not? How could techniques such as these assist a teacher in not breaking the class's momentum?

g. According to the teacher, she does not keep track of the students' progress on the token economies because she feels the students should self-monitor. Assess the validity of a teacher allowing students in the early elementary grades to self-regulate. What potential problems could exist?

5. Parent-Teacher Communication:

a. Evaluate Mrs. Boyd's approach to parent-teacher conferences. Discuss how her preconceived notions of parents' beliefs may have affected how she listened to parental concerns.

b. While Mrs. Boyd takes the time to explain her behavior management approaches to Harper's parents, she places a lot of emphasis on their student being the one responsible for communicating classroom procedures to her parents. Taking into account the age of the students in Mrs. Boyd's class, what possible difficulties might occur?

c. Mrs. Boyd does not offer explanations for why Harper has misunderstood the homework policy or the participation guidelines. Assess the importance of communicating classroom procedures and rules clearly both to students and parents.

d. Explain the importance for teachers to be able to alleviate parental concerns and to find a common ground in which both parents and teachers can work together for the benefit of the student.

e. Mrs. Boyd reflects on all the parent-teacher meetings that she has had with parents this year but does not consider altering her methods or giving merit to any of the parental concerns. Discuss the pros and cons of using reliable methods time after time versus evaluating techniques to include changes in the classroom dynamics or student populations.

f. In her conversation with Harper's parents, Mrs. Boyd does not offer solutions nor does she agree to assist Harper. What could Mrs. Boyd have done in this case to help Harper and other students who were not earning rewards?

g. Evaluate Mrs. Boyd's comment to Harper's parents at the end of their conference that Harper is likely to improve. Explain your answer.

Case 10

Handling Misbehavior and Student Excuses

Suggested Theories: Applications of Operant Conditioning, Effective use of Rewards and Punishment, Social Cognitive Theory and Modeling, Social Development, and Classroom Management
Teacher Challenges: Handling Student Misbehavior, Student Excuses, and Complaints
Student Level: Upper Elementary

Today is Logan's first day at his new school. After he and his mother check in at the front office, they begin to navigate the school hallways in search for Mrs. McAllister's fourth-grade classroom where he was assigned. The school is large, and students are going in all directions to their classes. Some students have formed groups and are chatting happily, while others are standing by themselves or sitting down reading a book or doodling on notebooks outside their classrooms. As Logan and his mother look for Mrs. McAllister's class, a group of boys run by and almost knock them over.

Before either he or his mother can react to what has occurred, they hear a male voice yell for the boys to stop running or they will be given an after-school detention. Logan feels a bit overwhelmed; after all, this is very different from what he was accustomed to. Logan and his family have just moved to this metropolitan city from their small town, where he attended a small school with children whom he had grown up with.

Logan and his mom enter Mrs. McAllister's classroom just as the class begins to fill with students. Students are walking over to hang up their book bags on the hooks on the far wall, and those students with lunchboxes are putting them on a neighboring shelf. They are then walking over to their seats and getting to work on what appears to be an activity that is on their desks. Mrs. McAllister smiles happily as she walks over to greet Logan and his mother. "Hi, I am Mrs. McAllister, it is lovely to meet you both! Welcome to my classroom! I am so happy you are joining us!"

Mrs. McAllister smiles and continues, "The students are working on a quiet activity which is part of our morning routine. At the end of the activity all students get the chance to put a classmate's name in the *Good Example Box* (she indicates to the large box by her desk), who they think has done a fabulous job demonstrating how all students should behave during that task. At the end of the month, students who were named in the *Good Example Box* will earn extra chances at the grab bag. You'll have a chance to nominate someone for the *Good Example Box* during another activity later today," Mrs. McAllister says and winks at Logan.

Logan surveys the room and sees many colorful charts and bulletin boards with students' work displayed on them. There are also bulletin boards with students' names on them and star stickers next to them—he can see that some students have more stars than others. Logan also sees a board that has a giant picture of what looks like a temperature gauge labeled *Behavior Meter*. It has colors ranging from the light blue at the bottom to fiery red at the top, and there are different student names on the various colors. Before he can continue his perusal of the room, his mother comes over to say goodbye and tells him to have a good day.

Mrs. McAllister introduces Logan to the class, and she explains to him that for the first week she has assigned him a helper to assist his getting acclimated to the class. Logan sees a girl waving for him to come over and sit by her. "Hi! I am Kailani," she exclaims excitedly and continues, "I'm your helper! Mrs. McAllister and I already went over my duties so I am ready to help! Your seat will be here. For this first week we have special permission to talk whenever we want, so be sure to ask me questions." She pats the seat next to her. Logan greets her as he sits down and unzips his book bag to take out his supplies.

Mrs. McAllister had sent his mom an email with the supplies he would need and other school information. Kailani smiles and says, "Oh good, you brought all your supplies; we lose recess if we aren't prepared for class. You can hang your book bag over on the hook. Your books are already in your desk. Our first subject of the day is math. We start math after our morning journal writing, which is the activity you just saw us do. We write in our journal about the topic that Mrs. McAllister assigns each morning, and we get to nominate a classmate for the *Good Example Box*. This paper here is where you would put someone's name and put it in the box.

"Okay, in math we are doing long-division. Open your book to page 56 and our assignment is to do problems 5–17. When Mrs. McAllister calls out *time*, she'll call some of us to the whiteboard to work them out." Logan thanks

Kailani and walks over to hang his backpack on the hook with his name on it and put his lunch box with the others. As Logan heads back to his desk, he notices that students have placed their homework on the edge of their desk. Mrs. McAllister is walking around checking it off in her grade book. Some students, he notices, are getting little star stickers and look pleased, while others are not.

After Mrs. McAllister finishes checking homework, the students who received stars are allowed to go to the star chart that Logan saw earlier and stick the star next to their name. As if guessing the direction of Logan's thoughts, Kailani says, "We have a star system in the class. Did you have that at your old school?" Logan shakes his head no, and Kailani explains, "Oh, it's not too hard to catch on to. Mrs. McAllister gives out star stickers for different things. Silver stars you can earn for assignments and homework."

Kailani then says, "At the end of each week, Mrs. McAllister will call out a number for silver stars—for example, six. If you have at least six silver stars, you get to choose an extra privilege from the privilege board—like siting with a friend, or eating lunch with the teacher, or choosing friends to play a board game during recess. But the fun part is that you never know how many silver stars you'll need each week, because Mrs. McAllister always changes the number . . . so you never know when you may get lucky! Now, the purple stars are for participation during class, and for every five purple stars you earn you get a chance at Mrs. McAllister's grab bag."

Kailani pauses and then continues, "Yellow stars can be earned for doing a good job on class chores, volunteering to help others, or demonstrating good behavior by not moving up in color on the *Behavior Meter*. We need three yellow stars to get a chance at the grab bag, which is filled with different school supplies and small toys." Kailani smiles and says in a lowered voice looking around the room, "Some kids hardly ever go to the grab bag and others go all the time, you'll see."

Mrs. McAllister has called a student up to her desk while the class works on their math assignment. "Addison, we discussed that looking at other students' papers to copy answers is breaking a class rule. We signed a class contract together ensuring that you knew you were breaking the rules, and we agreed that this behavior would not occur again. Yet, this is the third time this week that I have caught you looking at a classmate's paper or that a classmate has told me that you have tried to copy their work," Mrs. McAllister says sternly.

Addison, obviously upset, whines, "They're lying because they don't like me. I wasn't looking at anyone's paper, I was . . . um . . . reaching under my desk to get the pencil I dropped." Mrs. McAllister crosses her arms in front of her chest and replies unsympathetically, "You used a similar excuse when I caught you turned around in your seat during the grammar test. I believe you said it was a dropped eraser you were looking for, yet your answers matched closely to the answers of the student who was seated behind you. As we agreed in the contract, you have now lost all of the stars you earned this week and the chance to earn stars for the next week."

Addison puts her hands on either side of her face in surprise and cries out, "What! No! That is not fair! I worked hard for those stars! I told you I wasn't cheating!" Mrs. McAllister calmly says, "I don't want to hear any more on this subject or you are going to increase your punishment and lose recess. Now, please go and sit down and finish your work." Addison does return back to her desk while grumbling unhappily, but Logan sees she's not getting back to work on her math. In fact, she closes her math book, pushes it aside, and puts her head down.

"Okay class, please exchange papers with your neighbor so you can grade their paper. If I call your name, you know the drill . . . please come up to the whiteboard and start working on the problems." Mrs. McAllister calls out a list of names and directs each child to their assigned problem. As she looks out over the class, her attention immediately falls on two unruly students in the back of the room, and she quickly heads over to them. Logan turns around in his seat as Mrs. McAllister asks, "Gentlemen, is it correct behavior to push each other to reach the pencil sharpener first?" Both boys shake their heads and instantly offer justifications for their behavior.

"I do not want to hear all these explanations. You all know the correct way to behave. First thing this morning, I spoke to both of you because you entered the classroom arguing and both moved your colors from blue to yellow on the *Behavior Meter*—that was your warning which is what being on the color yellow means. Then the hall monitor informed me you were part of a group of kids that were running in the hallways before school started. You both moved your color from yellow to orange, and now with this misbehavior you'll both move to red; I'll send a note home and you'll both have to do a *Think About My Behavior Assignment* tonight," Mrs. McAllister says.

Logan leans over as they grade the math papers based on the answers on the board and asks Kailani in a whisper, "Have you ever had to do one of those *Think About My Behavior Assignments?*" "Nope, but I have seen them. It's a . . . um, what does she call them? Oh yes! A reflection writing assignment. So you have to write about what you did wrong, what class rules you broke, and what you should have done instead. Mrs. McAllister will only give you one if you have reached red on the *Behavior Meter*. By the way, make sure you know the class rules—they are posted by the entrance to the class," Kailani says and Logan nods.

Logan sees that Mrs. McAllister praises the students that got the problems correctly and happily awards them purple stars. The students that did not arrive at the correct answer, or needed her to assist them, do not earn a star. Those students team up with a "helper student" and head back to the classroom to the computer stations. Kailani explains that those students that need extra help go to the computers and the students helping them have a chance to earn yellow stars—so everyone loves to help.

Later, as the students line up for lunch, Mrs. McAllister asks Logan "How's it going? I see you and Kailani talking a lot, so I assume she is explaining things to you. She is a very good helper, but if you have any questions, please feel free to ask me, Okay?" Logan says,

"Yes, she's doing a great job. But it's lots to remember." Mrs. McAllister reassures him that while she expects he will abide by all the rules, she does expect he'll make mistakes in the first few weeks. Logan, as if suddenly realizing that they were headed to lunch, asks Mrs. McAllister nervously, "Where do I sit for lunch? Um, Kailani is not near me to ask her."

Mrs. McAllister puts her hand on Logan's shoulder caringly and replies, "There are no assigned seats at lunch; however, to help you with our lunch system, I have assigned two classmates to be your lunch buddies," Mrs. McAllister pauses to look to the boys in front of Logan and behind him in the boys' line and happily continues, "Great, I see that Ahmed and Jackson are right where they are supposed to be! Because we walk to lunch in two lines, a boy line and a girl line, I thought it easier to have Ahmed and Jackson be your lunch buddies. They're happy to do it, and they'll get yellow stars!" Jackson and Ahmed both nod cheerily.

Mrs. McAllister follows the boys to where they have shown Logan their class tables and adds, "Logan, your mom tells me that you really enjoy chess. Ahmed and Jackson are on our school's chess club, so I think you all would be a great fit together!" The boys begin opening their lunch boxes as Ahmed and Jackson pepper Logan with questions about his move and where he is from. Logan doesn't seem to mind the attention, and soon more students join the threesome. Mrs. McAllister doesn't usually accompany her students into the lunchroom, just to the doorway, as there are several lunch monitors who supervise students' lunch time.

However, today Mrs. McAllister lingers, ensuring that Logan is finding his way with the students assigned to help him. A problem arises at the hot lunch line when Addison and another student argue and shove one another, causing Addison's lunch to topple to the floor. Mrs. McAllister is certain she will be needing to address this issue back at the classroom. However, she is thrilled to see Logan has promptly gotten out of his seat to help Addison pick up the remnants of her lunch. Looks like her new student has earned his very first star, a yellow one, for his helping behavior! Mrs. McAllister is proud and can't wait to tell him this back in the classroom!

DISCUSSION QUESTIONS

1. Applications of Operant Conditioning:

   a. Explain how Skinner's theory of operant condition plays a role in this case. How can this theory be effectively applied to the classroom?

   b. How is the teacher in this case using reinforcers in her classroom? Are they effectively modifying student behavior? Identify potential hazards of a teacher overusing reinforcers?

   c. Distinguish between the different types of reinforcers that are employed in this case. Are all of the reinforcers used continuous ones? Positive reinforcers or negative reinforcers? Intrinsic reinforcers? Extrinsic reinforcers? How can using extrinsic reinforcers undermine the intrinsic value of a task for a student?

   d. Compare and contrast between the different intermittent schedules of reinforcement. Conclude how they differ from continuous reinforcement and discuss when it would be most effective for a teacher to use continuous reinforcement and when it would be best to use intermittent reinforcement.

   e. Which intermittent schedules of reinforcement does the teacher use in this case? Explain the schedule and the behavior the teacher is intending to reinforce by using this schedule.

   f. Explain the purpose of employing a contingency or behavior contract in the classroom. The teacher in the case uses one with a student; judge its effectiveness with regard to the student's behavior. Speculate on whether employing a contingency or behavior contract would have success on curbing a student's behavior.

   g. The teacher in this case is plagued with excuses from her students when they misbehave. Discuss how the teacher in this case tackles this issue and what role would *Think About My Behavior Assignments* play in assisting students to be more accountable for their behaviors.

2. Social Cognitive Theory:

   a. Describe how Bandura's social cognitive theory plays a role in this case. How can this theory be effectively applied to the classroom?

   b. Identify what the concept of modeling is for social cognitive theory and how students are affected by watching models? Are there occurrences of modeling in this case?

   c. Discuss how observational learning could be taking place in this case. Are all instances of observational learning ones that are positive learning experiences for the students in this classroom? Explain.

    d. Explain examples of vicarious reinforcement and vicarious punishment that take place in this case. Is the teacher intending for her students to learn vicariously?

    e. Determine how using a tactic such as the *Good Example Box* can have effects on a child's self-efficacy? Identify both positive and negative effects that this tactic could pose for self-efficacy?

    f. Outline how peer-tutoring and student helpers that the teacher has assigned as chores in her class could play a role in increasing the student's self-efficacy and self-regulation.

3. Social Development:

    a. A change in a child's environment such as moving can effect a child's social development. What measures does the teacher take to ensure that the new student in this case has an easier transition in her classroom and in the new school?

    b. Examine how the teacher's use of peer-tutors and student helpers in this class could aid a student's self-esteem and self-concept.

    c. Discuss how using tactics such as the *Good Example Box* can help to boost a child's self-esteem. What problems could teachers face with using these tactics that they would need to be aware of and plan for?

    d. The teacher in the case rewards not only academic behaviors but prosocial ones; identify examples where prosocial behaviors are rewarded and negative behaviors discouraged. How do her actions promote her students' social development?

4. Classroom Management:

    a. Identify this teacher's classroom management strategy, and discuss examples that support your answer.

    b. Conclude whether Mrs. McAllister demonstrates "withitness" in her classroom. What occurrences in this case speak to that? What makes a "desist" effective? In what ways does the teacher attempt to maintain academic momentum in her classroom?

    c. Is the classroom represented in this case study an example of an organized and equitable environment for the students?

    d. What classroom management techniques does Mrs. McAllister use when beginning her day and to maintain order during transitions?

    e. Explain how Mrs. McAllister uses the *Behavior Meter* to help students monitor their behavior. How could techniques such as these assist a teacher in not breaking the class's momentum?

    f. Outline examples of token economies that the teacher in this case is using and discuss their effectiveness on student behavior.

Case 11

Watch and Learn

The Teaching of Respect and Kindness

Suggested Theories: Social Cognitive Theory, Observational Learning, Modeling, Cognitive Development and Scaffolding, Social Development, and Memory

Teacher Challenges: Teaching Appropriate Classroom Behaviors, Class Clowns and Acting Out, Scaffolding Learners of Different Abilities, and Adequate Educational Supplies

Student Level: Kindergarten

It's Monday morning, and today is the deadline for the kindergarteners in Ms. Hayes's class to turn in the needed supplies for tomorrow's class project. Ms. Hayes posted the project's description and needed supplies, as well as its benefits to students' learning, on the class's website. She also sent several reminders of the upcoming due date for the supplies attached to her students' daily calendar. "Hi Ms. Hayes, here are the supplies! I remembered to bring them all by myself!" Samara says excitedly. "Oh thank you, Samara! Please tell your parents I appreciate it!" Ms. Hayes says.

As Ms. Hayes collects more supplies, Vanessa, a student seated in the back says loudly, "Ms. Hayes are the kids who didn't bring what they were supposed to still gonna get to do the project? My mom says it's not fair only kids that bring in the stuff should get to do the project! She's tired of being one of the parents that always sends stuff in—that's why my mom and Samara's mom and Kai's mom were talking about it at our drama class yesterday!" Ms. Hayes tries to appear unfazed at the outburst and replies, "If it is a class project then the entire class gets to participate in it."

Ms. Hayes closes the supplies closet and begins to collect the morning work from her students. The situation with the lack of supplies for projects is one that has her troubled, and though she would have preferred that Vanessa

85

not make that announcement to the class, she is aware that some parents are unhappy to be the ones always contributing to the class. Clearly, parents have now taken their discussions outside of the school.

To Ms. Hayes's dismay, it seems parents are showing their displeasure by stopping their contributions and possibly vocally encouraging other parents to do the same. This explains why some parents like Vanessa's and Kai's, who regularly contribute, are either decreasing their contributions or stopping all together. Ms. Hayes's class is large—at the top of what is allowed by the student/teacher ratio in the state—so without parental contributions for projects or extra funding from the school, which the administration has assured her is not possible, Ms. Hayes's students will not be doing very many projects.

"Okay. class, let's settle down and put on our listening ears on and silence ourselves so you can pay attention to the video we are going to watch. Remember, I told you all yesterday after math?" Ms. Hayes says as she tweaks her ears and places her finger over her mouth. Many students giggle but copy their teacher's gestures to indicate that they are ready for the video, and they nod their heads letting her know they remember. "Oh wonderful! I can see that Jeremiah is ready! Oh, and Rai and Tomas are also ready!" Ms. Hayes says enthusiastically as she surveys her students.

Ms. Hayes praises the ones that are sitting quietly with their arms resting on their desks and their fingers on their mouths. Many of the students look around to locate the children that Ms. Hayes calls on and alter their positions to match them. Once Ms. Hayes sees that all the students' attention is focused on her, she begins the educational video that she has purposely selected which centers on the importance of following class rules and being respectful. Ms. Hayes hopes that the video may help to reinforce that good behaviors lead to positive consequences.

Following the conclusion of the video, students are working on the activity that Ms. Hayes designed, which consists of cutting, coloring, and gluing pictures depicting scenes from the movie in sequential order onto brightly colored construction paper. Ms. Hayes has repeated the directions and has placed cue cards on the whiteboard to remind them of the steps. "Now class, what are some of the things we must remember as we cut out the pictures?" Ms. Hayes asks the class. "Yes, Peyton! I love how you raised your hand and waited to be called on! Good job!" Ms. Hayes says.

Peyton beams at the praise and says, "We need to cut carefully so we don't cut into the picture!" Ms. Hayes smiles nodding her head and says, "That is correct, Peyton! Now who can tell me some problems we can have with gluing or coloring?" Ms. Hayes sees that the amount of kids raising their hand instead of calling out has increased. "Yes Aaron? Thank you for raising your hand!" Aaron smiles proudly at the compliment and says sheepishly, "Do not put too much glue on the pictures . . . like I did last time! What a mess." Many children snicker but also nod their heads in agreement.

Ms. Hayes says she too agrees and prompts the class in recalling a time where they have all made that error. Ms. Hayes looks to the right to call on another student whose hand is up, but is interrupted by Clayton who suddenly shouts, "That you do not color too much on the picture, duh!" Many students giggle; however, Ms. Hayes shows her displeasure by saying firmly, "Why yes, that is true Clayton—but remember you need to wait to be called on before speaking and only use kind words." Ms. Hayes loves how well it works to use students as peer-models rather than having an adult do it.

As her students work, Ms. Hayes walks around to the students whose hands are raised indicating they need assistance. She first helps Peyton, who is having trouble putting some of the events in order. "Peyton, let's think, did the child in this picture perform the kind act before getting a sunflower patch or did he get the sunflower patch before he performed the kind act?" Ms. Hayes asks. Peyton thinks before quietly saying, "The kid did the kind act before getting the patch."

Ms. Hayes compliments her getting the answer so quickly, and after giving her a few more clues of the same nature on some of the other pictures, Peyton is able to complete the sequence. Students seated around Peyton are using Ms. Hayes's clues for Peyton to check their work and ensure that they are on the right track. Ms. Hayes notices it and says happily "Good job Jeremiah! I didn't have to tell you to fix the one picture you had out of order! You used the clue I gave Peyton to correct it yourself! You too, Kai!"

Ms. Hayes continues ensuring that students are on-track and upon seeing examples of good work, she continues extending praises. In a loud voice, Ms. Hayes exclaims, "Wow! Look how nicely Samara has cut her pictures! You cut right on the line and your entire picture shows nicely! Well done!" Students near Samara look over and begin to cut like her even going back to some of their previously cut pictures to confirm they are like Samara's. Ms. Hayes also compliments other students' gluing job and stresses that they are good examples of following directions.

When she hears students complimenting each other's work, she loudly praises their efforts in doing a kind act and modeling respect in the classroom. However, soon the forward momentum of the activity is stopped. "Stop telling me what color I should use on my pictures, Clayton! You're not the boss of me!" Vanessa says angrily. To which Clayton responds, "I was helping because your pictures look stupid! None of the kids had purple hair!" Ms. Hayes intervenes, has both students apologize, and discusses the importance of respect and kindness when expressing opinions, referencing the kids' actions in the video.

"Alright class, fabulous job on this activity! Now, as I call your table please place your completed work in your cubby to dry and line up for recess," Ms. Hayes says before allowing a few minutes to pass so students can clean up their desks. "Well, I love the way that Table 5 has put away all of their supplies and are quietly waiting. Table 5 may go!" Ms. Hayes says animatedly. The students in Table 5 are thrilled to be the first table called and happily begin walking to put away their projects. The rest of the class looks to see how the students in Table 5 were sitting and imitate them in hopes they'll go next.

"Wow! Tables 1 and 3 are doing great! Both of those tables may go!" Ms. Hayes says with a big smile. "Vanessa," Ms. Hayes calls out, "I appreciate your enthusiasm but remember we do not ever run in classroom, we always walk. Please go back to your seat and then try it again, and be sure to walk this time." Vanessa immediately stops and walks the rest of the way. Ms. Hayes sees that two other students who had begun to run have stopped and are slowly walking over to put their work away.

"Kai, all of your things just fell out of your cubby; you cannot line up and leave all of your belongings on the floor. Please go back and make sure your things are all in your cubby before lining up," Ms. Hayes says kindly, and Kai apologizes, saying she forgot that was a rule. As Kai replaces the fallen items back in the cubby, Ms. Hayes praises her and sees how other students whose items had fallen out of their cubbies are quickly putting them back before lining up. Ms. Hayes is getting ready to call the remaining two tables but has to stop to speak to Clayton who she sees is in line.

"Clayton, I have not called your table yet. Why are you in the line?" Ms. Hayes asks. "You didn't? Huh? I don't remember. But can't I just stay in line—I mean aren't ya going to call us anyways?" Clayton asks, seeming unpreoccupied with having broken the rules. Ms. Hayes doesn't answer Clayton right away, and instead calls the remaining two tables to put away their work and line up. "Well Clayton, you know the rules. Anyone who lines up before they are called gets to be the last person in line. Please step out of line and wait by me until all students have lined up," Ms. Hayes says strictly.

Later that day during reading time, Ms. Hayes is seated at a table in the back of the room helping her group of students who are struggling with this week's story. Ms. Hayes is frustrated that she hasn't been able to make much progress due to numerous interruptions to correct misbehaviors—she sighs when she hears chuckling coming from the direction of where Clayton is seated because she knows she'll have to address this situation before it worsens. She can see as she gets closer that Clayton has turned his hands into puppets, and he is telling jokes as if one hand puppet was talking to the other.

As usual he has succeeded in distracting all of the classmates seated around him, as they are all paying attention to his antics rather than doing their work. "Clayton, is this how you are supposed to behave?" Ms. Hayes asks in a strict tone. Clayton looks up at her and says defiantly, "I was just telling jokes from the book I checked out from the library. You said I could read a book if I finished early. I'm done early, soooo I'm readin'—ta da!" Clayton finishes making a big show of waving his hands in the air like a magician would do after a trick—a gesture the majority of the students in class instantaneously laugh at.

Ms. Hayes is not pleased. "Clayton, you're disrupting the class, and I have already warned you once today. Please go and sit in the *Thinking Spot* until I call you," Ms. Hayes says indicating the back corner of the classroom. Ms. Hayes's *Thinking Spot* is an area she has set up in order to have students go there after a misbehavior so they can consider making better choices. The student is reminded of the class rules while in the *Thinking Spot*, because there is a copy of them on the wall, as well as illustrations the students have made that depict examples of the class rules.

Clayton is a frequent visitor to the *Thinking Spot*, as are a few others. However, it's often difficult to predict whether or not it will be effective because Clayton doesn't always curb his behavior even after having thought about it. His disruptions are troubling to Ms. Hayes because Clayton is very well liked by his classmates, and it seems that it is their attention he is seeking, not hers. In addition, Ms. Hayes has noticed that his negative behavior and the attention he receives from his classmates are encouraging other students in the class who do not normally misbehave to act out.

Ms. Hayes is definitely concerned because her class consists of students with varying abilities. Some students, like Clayton, need very little guidance in completing their work, but others need a considerable amount of support. As such, it is crucial that all students get used to working quietly and independently to allow Ms. Hayes to attend to the varying needs of all students. Ms. Hayes was sure that the daily activity sheets and various reading options she designed for the students who finish their work early would work at keeping them engaged and focused; however, this doesn't seem to be the case.

As if on cue, Jeremiah says, pointing in the direction of the *Thinking Spot*, "Look Ms. Hayes! Clayton is trying a stunt!" Ms. Hayes turns to look at Clayton who, while in the *Thinking Spot*, has clearly gotten out of his seat to grab colored pencils from a nearby bin. He is standing up dancing and making funny faces while holding the colored pencils at the top of his head like they are horns.

DISCUSSION QUESTIONS

1. Social Cognitive Theory:

   a. Describe how the teacher is using Bandura's social cognitive theory in her classroom.
   b. Identify examples of observational learning that are taking place in this case. What types of models are students being exposed to in this

case? According to social cognitive theory, how are students' behavior affected by watching models?

  c. Determine whether all the instances of observational learning are positive learning experiences for the students in this classroom? Discuss examples in the case of inhibition/disinhibition. Is the teacher intending to use this concept? Why or why not?

  d. Identify and explain examples in this case where you think that response facilitation has taken place. Is the teacher intending to use this concept? Why or why not?

  e. Explain examples of vicarious reinforcement and vicarious punishment that take place in this case. Is the teacher intending for her students to learn vicariously? Why or why not?

  f. How are the parents of the students in this case possibly being influenced by other parents' reactions to bringing extra school supplies?

  g. Determine how using a tactic such as the *Thinking Spot* can have positive effects on a child's self-regulation? Identify both positive and negative effects that this tactic could pose for self-regulation.

  h. How does using a tactic like the *Thinking Spot* relate to time-out as a form of punishment? How can using time-outs in the classroom be used effectively? Outline how the teacher's use of praise as is seen in the case could help boost a student's self-efficacy.

2. Social Development:

  a. The students in the case are young and as such are having trouble with various social aspects. How do the teacher's actions assist in their learning of what is and is not socially acceptable?

  b. Examine how the teacher's lack of harsh punishments and overall encouraging tone could aid a student's social-emotional development. How does children's emotional self-regulation improve during these ages?

  c. Discuss how using tactics such as the *Thinking Spot* can help to boost a child's self-esteem. What problems could teachers face with using these tactics that they would need to be aware of and plan for?

  d. The teacher in the case rewards not only academic behaviors but prosocial ones; identify examples where prosocial behaviors are rewarded and negative behaviors discouraged. How do her actions promote her students' social development?

3. Cognitive Development:

  a. According to Piaget, identify the stage of cognitive development that the students are likely to be in.

b. Explain how Piaget's concept of egocentrism is apparent in this case. Identify strategies for how teaches can help students to appreciate the perspective of others, including their peers.

c. Discuss instances in the case which involves Vygotsky's concept of the zone of proximal development.

d. How is the teacher in this case attempting to handle students' various zones of proximal development? What struggles is she encountering?

e. Explain how scaffolding is demonstrated in this case. Is the teacher engaging in scaffolding effectively? What are other ways this teacher might scaffold students' learning?

f. How could the teacher improve on the *Thinking Spot* idea in her class by including more direct scaffolding?

g. Outline the benefits that using student models and student-generated ideas as take place in this case influence students' actions.

4. Memory:

a. Describe the role that students' attention is playing a role in this case. Is the teacher assisting her students' in paying attention? How so?

b. Discuss how the teacher's use of *listening ears* and *silence ourselves* in conjunction with gestures assist students' attention to stay focused.

c. The teacher in this case is having a problem keeping the students from paying attention to Clayton, the class clown. From the role of attention, how can a teacher handle this situation?

d. Generate examples of the learning strategies that the teacher in this case uses to assist her students in remembering tasks. What other strategies could teachers employ?

e. At what ages are students becoming metacognitive learners? What are early learning and monitoring strategies that elementary teachers will begin to teach young students?

f. Discuss examples in this case that demonstrate student's long-term memory? How does the teacher employ the use of retrieval cues? How does the teacher employ visual imagery to help her students remember the rules while in the *Thinking Spot*?

g. What instances show the children forgetting? Would forgetting play a common role for kindergarteners? Why or why not?

Case 12

Preparing Twenty-First-Century Learners

Teaching Students to Think

Suggested Theories: Information processing and Memory, Learning Strategies and Metacognition, Social Cognitive Theory, Operant Conditioning, and Behavior Modification
Teacher Challenges: Teaching Thinking and Study Skills, Students Dominating Discussions
Student Level: Upper Elementary School

"Hello there, my favorite fifth-graders," Mr. Villanueva says as he greets his students by the door, "How was lunch?" Most students say hello and reply that they enjoyed their lunch time with friends. "As you get settled in to your seats, please notice our lesson for today that is up on the screen at the front of the class. We will be continuing our discussing of the solar system and some of the properties of each planet."

Mr. Villanueva also takes a moment to quietly ask Marcus a question as he makes his way in. "Marcus, did you bring me back the note I gave you yesterday to take home?" "Oh, no!" Marcus cries out and says, "I totally forgot to take it home with me because I left my science folder in my locker! Sorry Mr. V." The teacher guides the student out of the incoming lunch traffic before continuing sternly, "You know Marcus, I even reminded you yesterday before you left to go to the car line to get picked up by your mom. It is important one of your parents sign off on that letter. I am asking them to come in for a parent conference."

"I know Mr. V., and I walked to the car line trying to remind myself, you know? But then I don't know what happened, 'cause I must have forgot," Marcus says in an apologetic tone. "Well, Marcus I am giving you one last chance to return the note to me; otherwise, I am going to have to call your parents," Mr. Villanueva states.

"I get it, Mr. V. I will write it down on my planner again, and you know what? My sister always moves her bracelets from the hand she always wears them on to the other hand to help her remember. So why don't I put a post-it in my lunchbox so that it will help me remember, that always works for my mom," replies Marcus. Mr. Villanueva nods at Marcus and heads to the front of the class to begin the day's lesson on the last planet the class will be studying before their review for the exam on the solar system.

With about half of the class time left, Mr. Villanueva begins the class on a review for their upcoming unit test on the solar system. "Okay class, let's begin reviewing for our test, remember for the next two days we will be reviewing so now is the time to ask questions on information that may not be clear to you," Mr. Villanueva says. Most of the students turn their notebooks to a new page to copy down notes. As he begins the review, he walks over to a cardboard cutout that is folded in half and leaning against the side chalkboard and brings it over to display it in front of the class.

The board is a huge representation of the solar system, with the planets made out of soft foam and thus appearing three dimensional. "Alright class, remember this is what our universe looks like, well, of course the real universe is much larger, and of course the planets are not made out of foam!" The class laughs. "Of course we remember that board, Mr. V! It is sooo big and has so much color and stuff on it!" Jackie says pointedly. "Oh good, so tell me what is the first planet in our solar system?" Mr. Villanueva asks and nods at Todd a student in the back who has his hand raised. "Mercury," Todd hesitantly answers.

"Right Todd," Mr. Villanueva replies and continues his inquiry, "and so what are the other three inner planets?" Mr. Villanueva nods at Leticia who has her hand raised. "Um, Venus, Earth and . . ." Leticia answers and hesitates for a moment on the last planet. "It is characteristically known as the red planet," Mr. Villanueva offers Leticia. "Oh, it is Mars! I remember because red is my favorite color," Leticia excitedly says. "Yes, Mars is correct, Leticia. . . . Like how you came up with a personal way to remember that!"

Mr. Villanueva then asks the class, "What else do we know about Mars?" "That its climate is dry and cold, kind of like it is here," says Jackie and many students laugh. "Right, very good you remember that," Mr. Villanueva says grinning. "Mars also has a thin atmosphere," Jackie continues. "Yes!" Mr. Villanueva exclaims and asks, "What is Mars's atmosphere made up of?" While he see Jackie wanting to answer, he knows her penchant to dominate the discussion, so he quickly interjects, "Let's hear from someone else." "Carbon, um, monoxide—no, I mean carbon dioxide," says Miguel as he blushes.

"That is Okay Miguel, it is an easy mistake to make because the two are very close, so I am impressed that you could remember the difference and correct your mistake." Miguel nods and smiles at Mr. Villanueva as he looks down at his desk. "Okay so what else do we know about Mars?" Mr. Villanueva asks the class. "That every year it has dust storms that affect the whole planet. I remember that because I am allergic to dust," Marcus says. Jackie replies "Wow, you must sneeze a lot." "Yeah!" Marcus replies and many students laugh. "Alright, how many satellites are there on Mars?" Mr. Villanueva asks the class.

"Two," Jackie proudly replies. "That is right!" Mr. Villanueva says and continues, "Now, someone who hasn't answered yet, can you remember their names?" "Isn't one called phobia?" asks Matthew. "No, what a derpy answer, that is a fear of something you dork!" says Jackie and the class laughs. "Yeah, like living in a place like Mars! Can you imagine?" Natalie asks. "No, because it would be creepy, I mean there is no life on Mars, right Mr. V.?" Abby asks.

"No Abby, there is no life on Mars today, although there is speculation that at one time the conditions might have allowed for it because runoffs of water were discovered," Mr. Villanueva says and continues, "The name of the satellite is Phobos, so you were close, Matthew—and no name-calling, Jackie." "Sorry Mr. V.," Jackie says. Mr. Villanueva nods at Jackie to acknowledge her apology. "The other satellite is called Deimos, it's the smaller of the two, right Mr. V.?" says Todd. "Correct! Great review of Mars, class!" Mr. Villanueva shares, genuinely pleased with the amount of introductory planetary information kids seemed to have absorbed.

This, Mr. Villanueva thinks, will be an important foundation to build on later in the course. "Now, I am going to pass around another review activity I want you to take home and work on. This worksheet has some important questions reflective of our unit on the planets. See how much you know and can fill out on your own. It's a great way to self-assess your understanding and to know what parts you need to spend more time to study on. Then, you can set some goals for your studying at home to be best prepared on the day of the test. Are there any questions?" Mr. Villanueva asks. "Is Mars the only planet on the test?" asks Jackie.

"No Jackie, please remember that the test is on the entire solar system, and we will review all of the planets before the test," Mr. Villanueva replies. "Yeah, I usually just repeat it over and over again until it just gets into my brain," states Marcus. "That is good, but also do not forget to remember to build on the new information by connecting it to information you already know, like Leticia did earlier with the color red," says Mr. Villanueva. "Oh yeah, good idea," Marcus replies.

"Do we have to know all of the stuff about each one and also the order they go in? Because I am not that good with that, I always remember the first planet we covered, as well as the ones we just talked about, but the others all just sorta run together in my mind," Natalie states worriedly. "Yes, you will have to know all of the planets and their order and actually for tonight's homework, I want you to create a mnemonic sentence by using the first letter of each of the planets in the solar system order to help with your review. Tomorrow we will share our sentences with each other, and I will tell you one that always works for me," states Mr. Villanueva. Matthew replies, "No Mr. V., tell us yours now." "No, no, I would like to give you the chance to construct your own using your own experiences Okay?" replies Mr. Villanueva, and Matthew moves as to begin pestering him good-naturedly, but at that moment the bell rings. "Great! There's the bell, class, so you are dismissed!" The students quickly pack up their belongings and head toward the door.

DISCUSSION QUESTIONS

1. Information Processing and Memory:

   a. Identify examples in this case that depict episodic memory.
   b. Relate examples in this case that depict semantic memory.
   c. Generate examples in this case that depict explicit memory.
   d. Identify examples in this case of short-term memory use. What limitations exist in short-term/working memory? Discuss at least one limitation demonstrated in this case.
   e. How do the students in Mr. Villanueva's class demonstrate the use of long-term memory?
   f. Explain rehearsal in long-term memory? Describe an instance in the case in which rehearsal is being employed.
   g. Explain the serial positioning effect? Which student in the case is showing evidence of having this problem?

2. Learning Strategies and Metacognition:

   a. How does forming images aid our retrieval of information? Is the use of visual imagery present in this case? Can you come up with additional examples the teacher might use in teaching about the solar system?
   b. Discuss what meaningful learning is. How does it differ from rote memorization? Discuss instances in the case of meaningful learning.
   c. Elaborations aid our memory; summarize how elaborations are used in this case.
   d. Identify mnemonics demonstrated in this case? What is the advantage of using mnemonics?

e. Recount how Mr. Villanueva employs retrieval cues in this case? How do retrieval cues aid our recall of information?

f. Mr. Villanueva presents information in an organized manner, how does organization aid our memory? Generate other types of organization that you could use in the classroom to aid your students' learning and recall of material?

g. How can teachers encourage students' study skills? What is metacognition?

h. What are effective learning and monitoring strategies this teacher might suggest for students?

i. What evidence in the case do we see of peer-modeling of learning strategies? And how might teachers encourage peer-modeling of adaptive metacognitive strategies?

j. How can teachers best utilize self-assessment in their classrooms?

k. What tips would you share with your own students about ways to set goals to manage their own self-directed learning?

3. Social Cognitive Theory:

a. Identify what the concept of modeling is for social cognitive theory and how students are affected by watching models? Are there occurrences of modeling in this case?

b. What is self-regulated learning, and what evidence in the case do you see this relate to? What do theorists mean when they refer to the self-regulated learning cycle?

c. What role might goal-setting play within self-regulation?

d. What role might self-assessment play within self-regulation? How can teachers use self-assessment activities to encourage students' adaptive learning strategies?

e. What overlap do you see between the concepts of metacognition and that of self-regulation?

f. How might teachers encourage students' self-regulatory skills? What role might parents play? How can homework be used as a vehicle to practice these skills?

g. What are some examples of how you use self-regulatory strategies to further your own learning?

4. Operant Conditioning and Behavior Modification:

a. Distinguish between different types of positive reinforcers that are being used in this case. Discuss its effectiveness on modifying behavior.

b. Relate instances in which Mr. Villanueva uses punishment? If so, how does he employ it? Is it successful?

   c. Analyze how teachers employ reinforcement and punishment effectively. Support your answer.

   d. What about those students who constantly dominate class discussion?
Was the teacher effective at handling these disturbances? And if not,
what suggestions would you make?

Part IV

MOTIVATION

Case 13

When Rewards Backfire

Suggested Theories: Extrinsic and Intrinsic Motivation, Achievement Goals, and Parent Involvement
Teacher Challenges: Misuse of Extrinsic Rewards, Undermining Intrinsic Motivation, Student Interruptions to Instruction, and Communicating with Concerned Parents
Student Level: Upper Elementary

Mr. Bennett has instructed his fifth-grade class from the very start that those who score a 90% on the multiple-choice unit tests would each earn a no homework pass. Mr. Bennett felt this reinforcer would work with all students. Students were genuinely excited, and the rewards had been quite effective so far in motivating students to really apply themselves in class. It is now the second month of the school year, and Mr. Bennett is about to introduce the lesson on world continents. He waits for the students as they begin to settle down and turn their attention to the front of the class.

He smiles and then begins, "Okay class, now that I have your attention, I'd like to introduce our next unit titled 'World Continents.' I am sure you are going to enjoy this topic. World geography has always been one of my favorite areas of study. So, if you will now turn to page—" Interrupting the teacher, a student named Rachel exclaims, "Wait a minute Mr. Bennett! Why do we have to learn about places half way across the world? I don't care about places I am never gonna get to see. What's the point?"

Mr. Bennett looks pointedly at the student and responds, "Rachel, I don't like to discourage student questions, but you know what our class rule is about talking out of turn. You have to raise your hand first. Besides, this is a very important lesson. There will be an important test at the end of the week on this material. So, I suggest we get to work."

Later the same day the class is involved in a cooperative learning activity. One group of students is talking about the upcoming unit test. "I don't know about all of you, but I am going to study real hard for the test on Friday. I would really like another homework pass. I hate having to do homework all the time. There's so much of it!" Amelia shares.

Another student named Lydia offers a different perspective. "My mom doesn't care much anyway as long as I keep up my test grades and stuff. Besides, I am much better at the presentations Mr. Bennett has us do. You know, where we get to make charts and pictures and stuff? I am great at putting that stuff together on my computer at home." Amelia nods her head excitedly in agreement. "So," Lydia continues, "I don't care about those passes. Now a pizza party, that would have been a really cool."

Amelia shakes her head and states, "Well, it's not like you have to study all that much. You don't have to get a perfect score to get the pass, just a ninety. What about you Luis?" Luis pauses before responding, "I don't know. It's cool and everything. But it only gets you out of one little assignment. Besides, I get a pass every week. It won't be a big deal if I don't get it this time." Another student, Sharice, nods in agreement, "Don't get me wrong, I can see how everyone likes them and all. But this stuff is kinda cool. I don't know that much about people in other parts of the world. The homework gives me a chance to learn more about all the countries."

It is three days later and Mr. Bennett has just concluded the opening lesson on Asia. A student named Jesse shares his interest: "Wow, Mr. Bennett, that was really cool! When do we hear about Europe? That's where all those kings and queens lived, right? Do you think we will get to see pictures on the internet of these places?" This catches Luis's attention, who says, "What are you talking about Jesse? What kings and queens? Did they live in big castles and all that? Boy, would I love to see that. I saw this show one time that . . ."

At this point, Mr. Bennett interjects. "Now wait guys, you know we have to turn to our next activity. However, we will continue our discussion on the continents tomorrow. So, I would appreciate everyone pulling out your list of spelling words."

It is Monday morning before the class has started, and Mr. Bennett is reviewing his roll book. He notices that students' grades have been good and decides it may be time to start weaning the kids off the extrinsic rewards this week. Students are starting to file in and he gets up to start the class. "Class, as usual I am proud of all you who got an 'A' on this week's test. However, next week we're going to do something a little different. Only those students who get a perfect score will receive the no homework pass. You have all been doing so well, I feel it is time to 'up the ante,' so to speak." Noticeable groans occur throughout the class.

"That's not fair, Mr. Bennett. What about those of us who do pretty good? We're not going to get anything?" complains Amelia. Another student, Derek, agrees, "Yeah, I agree with Amelia. What are we gonna get instead? Some of us just can't get the best scores all the time." (At this point the whole class starts talking about this new state of affairs, and Mr. Bennett is a little concerned about his decision to alter the criteria.) Mr. Bennett seems a bit unsure about the class' reaction but proceeds, "Well, class, I am not sure about that. Let's just try this new plan for now."

Two weeks have passed, and Mr. Bennett is growing more concerned about how many of the students are responding to the change in criteria that earns the no homework pass. Many are visibly upset when he hands out the homework passes. He has also noticed that not as many students are earning the pass, and grades have noticeably dropped on the last two tests. He has even received phone calls from upset parents who feel the new criteria are unfair because their children are at a disadvantage for earning class incentives.

So Mr. Bennett decides to consult some of his colleagues during his planning period in the faculty lounge. "I thought I was doing everything right. You start the rewards off generously and then wean them off, right? Isn't that what those schedules of reinforcement are all about?" Another teacher, Mr. Murphy, shakes his head knowingly, "Well, I hear you. From the start of the school year, I have kids who expect some kind of return on their learning. If I introduce an assignment or project they ask 'What's in it for me?'"

Another teacher named Mrs. Payne who has been following the conversation hesitates and then offers her opinion. "Personally, I respect that other teachers use such incentives to motivate their students, but I wonder if they aren't overused so much so that kids rely on them. They don't seem to get the concept of learning for the sake of learning."

Mr. Bennett has listened attentively to this exchange but now becomes more animated. "Well, do you think I should have been more sparing in my use of rewards? I still think the no homework pass is a good idea because it worked so well in the beginning. The trouble started when I made the criteria for earning the pass more difficult." Mrs. Payne replies, "Maybe the students see the tougher criteria as unfair? Maybe this only allows the higher ability students the opportunity to earn the reward?"

Mr. Bennett tries to rein in his frustration before replying, "That's exactly what some of my students' parents have complained about! I have even noticed that this whole troublesome issue has led to interruptions during instruction time, and I know I am going to have to set up at least a few parent-teacher conferences! What should I do now?"

DISCUSSION QUESTIONS

1. Effective Use of External Rewards:

    a. Discuss the teacher's misuse of extrinsic motivation. What suggestions might you offer for a more judicious use of extrinsic motivation?
    b. What are diverse types of reinforcement that teachers can make use of in the classroom? What is a reinforcement menu?
    c. What are schedules of reinforcement? Designate which schedules a teacher should use to reduce the likelihood of extinction of desirable behavior.
    d. Assess the pros and cons of using external reinforcers in the classroom? Should students be rewarded for learning?
    e. Evaluate the argument surrounding whether homework passes should be used in the classroom as a reward?

2. Intrinsic Motivation:

    a. Are there any lost opportunities on the teacher's part where he should have capitalized on students' intrinsic motivation in the lesson? What suggestions might you offer that include opportunities for nurturing students' intrinsic motivation.
    b. Determine what role classroom technology can play in encouraging students' intrinsic motivation to learn.
    c. How can humor, personal experiences, and anecdotes show the human side of academic content and foster intrinsic motivation?
    d. What original sources can Mr. Bennett expose his students to in order to communicate important academic content while sparking student interest?
    e. Suggest ways that teachers can allow for student choice in their learning given curriculum constraints.

3. Goal Orientations:

    a. What are mastery and performance goals? What goals do you see evidence for in this case?
    b. Evaluate whether performance goals are always bad. What is the difference between a performance-approach goal and a performance-avoidance goal?
    c. Evaluate whether mastery goals are always beneficial. What is the difference between a mastery-approach goal and a mastery-avoidance goal?
    d. How might the teacher's classroom structure have influenced such motivational patterns?

e. How can teachers structure the classroom to create more adaptive achievement goals in their students? How do the nature of learning tasks, evaluation and assessment measures, and classroom climate impact students' goals? What does TARGET stand for in looking at students' motivation to learn in school?

4. Classroom Management:

   a. Do you think Mr. Bennett is "withit"? Do you think he uses desists effectively? How would you evaluate his ability to maintain academic focus in his classroom? How might teacher demonstrate more "withitness"?
   b. Following how case developed, is this a teacher-owned, student-owned, or owned-by-both problem according to TET? What suggestions would follow from TET as to resolving this dilemma?
   c. How can behavioristic strategies be utilized so all students have the opportunity to earn rewards while also improving classroom management? Ascertain how extrinsic rewards might be utilized in a more comprehensive classroom management approach in Mr. Bennett's class?
   d. Explain the role of establishing classroom rules and procedures under the Marzano teacher evaluation model. Do you think the teacher has done a thorough job in this respect? Why or why not?

5. Parent Involvement:

   a. How might home-school communication be of benefit in this case? How can home-school partnerships impact student motivation to learn?
   b. Identify effective ways to facilitate home-school communication.
   c. Develop a list of tips for effective parent-teacher conferencing.
   d. Recommend how a teacher might go about increasing parents' involvement in their child's schooling.

Case 14

Caught in the Middle

Children of Divorce

Suggested Theories: Maslow's Hierarchy of Needs, Motivation, Social Development, and Bronfenbrenner's Ecological Theory

Teacher Challenges: Behavioral Challenges due to Changes in Home Environment, Trouble Engaging Children of Divorce, and Changes in Home Environment that affect Student's Social Development

Student Level: Upper Elementary

Ms. Zimmerman is sitting at her desk attaching field-trip form reminders to her first-grade students' take-home folders while her students are in physical education. The students are thrilled to be going on their field trip to the Science Museum next week, and Ms. Zimmerman has been planning a series of activities that go along with what the children will be learning. However, as part of any field trip, the students must bring in their signed parental consents, and she is particularly concerned about one of her students, Landon, returning the field-trip form.

Landon's parents recently divorced, and he alternates his time between being with his mother and being with his father. Ms. Zimmerman is cognizant of the challenges that this may bring and always tries to alert both parents of the class's requirements; unfortunately, communication on her part alone doesn't mean complications can be prevented.

Landon's turn to be student of the week is this week and just like all of the other students, Landon was ecstatic to have his turn. The students love the opportunity to engage in a few special classroom privileges such as sitting in the teacher's chair, being first to line up, and getting to choose where they sit daily. Additionally, the child of the week gets to have their unique abilities, talents, and likes displayed in their *All About Me* poster that they complete with the help of their parents. And they get to bring in a special item every day that they get to show the class at the beginning of the day.

It is nearing the end of the week and, while Landon has enjoyed his classroom privileges as student of the week, he has not brought in his *All About Me* poster and has only been able to share one item with the class all week. Ms. Zimmerman always sends the announcement for student of the week in the children's take-home folder the week before allowing parents extra time to work on the project; in addition, with Landon's parents, she also sent them an email.

This morning when Ms. Zimmerman asked Landon about his poster and if he had brought in anything to show, Landon responded disappointedly, "My mom's been at work 'til late and she's really busy with the move. My dad told me he was sorry he couldn't help me because he's away . . . for his work." Ms. Zimmerman was surprised to hear Landon was moving, to which he replied sadly, "Yeah, not my dad, just my mom and my brother and my sister and me. When we are with my mom, we'll now be living with my mommy's boyfriend . . . so can't get my stuff because it's packed in boxes."

Ms. Zimmerman offers to give Landon another chance to be student of the week later in the year; however, Landon shrugs his shoulders and appears disinterested. Ms. Zimmerman worries about the toll that moving will take on Landon. He is already often late to school, forgets homework and school books, and he is continuously distracted—his attention seems to always be on something other than school. Landon's kindergarten teacher is a friend of Ms. Zimmermans, and she shared with her that prior to Landon's family going through the divorce, Landon was one of her best students—always motivated and happy, well-adjusted, and well-behaved.

During physical education, Landon's class is playing dodge ball; students that have already been tagged are sitting down watching the game. "Hey Landon, why didn't you come to the park with us yesterday?" Dominic asks. "What? You all went to the park yesterday?" Landon asks, clearly hurt he'd not gone. "Yeah! But my dad said he couldn't get a hold of your dad," Dominic replies. "Oh no, he's away and I was at my mom's house . . . and um, she, I mean we, live farther away now," Landon replies as he looks down at his sneakers, clearly uncomfortable with the subject.

"Wait, you moved?" Dominic asks surprised. "No, not when I'm with my dad. Then I'm still in the same neighborhood, but when I'm with my mom we moved far. . . . We moved in with Frank, her boyfriend . . . I . . ." Landon answers, but before he can finish his sentence, Christian, who is walking over to the group after having gotten out of the game, says sneeringly, "Your mom has a boyfriend! Ooooo . . . she is in loooovvvveeee!"

A few other kids that overheard the comment start laughing, and Landon's demeanor changes from being uncomfortable to confrontational. "Shut up

Christian! Don't make fun of my mom!" Landon shouts as he pushes Christian. Christian shouts, "Hey! Don't push me!" as he shoves Landon back, and the boys enter a pushing and shouting match. Coach Melendez runs over to separate the boys.

A few hours later, Landon's class is in lunch and its Maya's birthday that day, so her mom has come in with cupcakes to share with the class. "Hi Landon," Maya's mom says warmly as she puts a nicely decorated cupcake with a butterfly ring in front of him. "I hope you are going to be able to come to Maya's birthday party this weekend. I haven't heard from your parents on whether or not you are attending. The whole class is invited—it will be very fun!" Landon shifts anxiously in his seat and says quietly, "I dunno yet, I can't remember if I am at my mom or my dad's this weekend."

Maya's mother immediately understands and answers kind-heartedly, "Oh no problem, I'll give them a call to remind them then! We hope you can make it!" Landon continues to eat his lunch, but gives his cupcake to Dominic, who's sitting next to him, because he doesn't feel much like eating it. "Hey thanks!" Dominic replies excitedly and then gives half of it to Jose, laughing at his friend's pleading expression to share the extra cupcake. "How come you don't want it?" Samuel asks from across the table.

Landon just shrugs his shoulder in response. "It's really good!" Jose adds around a mouthful of cupcake. "I got an idea for the party, why don't you come with me, Dominic, and Jose to the party? I'm sure my mom wouldn't mind bringing you too—you're just down the street!" Samuel says excitedly while Jose adds in, "I can't wait to go! It's at that cool new party place!" "Yeah! That's a great idea!" answers Dominic elatedly. Landon smiles though he looks skeptical; nevertheless he responds with little enthusiasm, "Guess I'll ask."

After lunch, Ms. Zimmerman's class is playing at recess and she notices that Landon is not playing with the other children. What's more concerning is that she sees that several of his friends have attempted to have him join them, but he seems uninterested. "Hi Landon, are you feeling Okay?" Ms. Zimmerman asks caringly. "Yeah," Landon answers while he looks down at his hands. "Oh well, that's good to hear. I just wondered why you aren't playing?" Ms. Zimmerman asks as she sits next to him on the bench. "I dunno, guess I don't feel like playing football," Landon answers dejectedly as he looks over to his friends tossing the ball to each other.

"Oh, I thought you liked football? Didn't you play on a team?" Ms. Zimmerman asks. "Um yeah, I do like it . . . yeah, I did play. Me and Dominic were on the same team, but, well, I didn't get to play this season because my mom couldn't take time off work to take me. Same thing will happen with baseball, because now that we moved in with my mom's boyfriend we're too far away for me to play on the team with my friends." Ms. Zimmerman nods in understanding and says, "I can see why that would make you sad, but at school you still have your friends right? And when you start playing on teams where you live now you'll make new friends."

The next day during math, Landon's mind wanders back to Maya's party. He doesn't think either of his parents has returned Maya's mom messages, even though he told them how much he wanted to go to the party. Landon looks out the classroom window and sighs. He's so tired of skipping parties and playdates with his friends. He's not even able to ride his bike and play in the neighborhood park after school with his friends like he used to, because he's not at his dad's all that much and that's the neighborhood that is close to the school.

"Landon," Ms. Zimmerman calls, out snapping him out of his thoughts, "do you know the answer to the problem? Are you paying attention? Where is your math workbook? It should be on your desk while we go over the homework problems. Did you leave it at home again?" Ms. Zimmerman asks gently standing over him. Landon is surprised to see her standing in front of his desk—wasn't she by the whiteboard—Landon looks at his empty desktop and stammers a reply, "Um . . . yes, I must have . . . I . . . couldn't find it in my book bag."

Ms. Zimmerman sighs and says, "Okay, share with Maya, but please try to remember your supplies tomorrow. You also did not bring your spelling homework, and the librarian just told me your library book is overdue by a few weeks. Now let's focus on the lesson, Okay?" Landon nods as he fights back the tears. All the switching from his mom to his dad's makes it so hard to remember which days he is with which parent and his things are hard to keep track of.

He sees Christian staring at him from across the room with a satisfied smile on his face before saying proudly, "I know the answer, Ms. Zimmerman, my homework is right here on my desk!" Maya, who is sitting next to Landon, moves her book as instructed so she and Landon can share. However, Landon pushes her book away making it fall of the desk with a loud sound and yells, "Keep your book! I don't want to do this anyway!" The students are all startled by the disruption and Ms. Zimmerman must stop the lesson once again to handle the situation with Landon.

The day of the field trip has arrived, and Ms. Zimmerman reflects on the fun activities that her students got to partake while at the Museum of Science. Although it was an enriching experience for the students, the day was unfortunately not without its difficulties, primarily for Landon. Ms. Zimmerman had asked that all students wear their school-pride T-shirts on the field trip as is customary and had placed a reminder in yesterday's home folder. The school requires that students all have school-pride T-shirts and the information for ordering additional school-pride T-shirts is on the school's webpage as well as on Ms. Zimmerman's class website.

Landon was the only student who had come to school not wearing his school-pride T-shirt, and he began to cry when he realized it. Ms. Zimmerman comforted him and assured him the field trip would still be very fun. He was unfortunately disappointed once again when they arrived at the museum and he realized he was not in Samuel and Dominic's group as they were with Dominic's mom, who was one of the parents volunteering. Ms. Zimmerman always allows the students whose parents are chaperoning to choose two other students they want in their group, and Dominic had chosen Samuel and Jose to be in his group.

Ms. Zimmerman is heading home after the school day making a quick stop by the office to drop off some paperwork and runs into Chet Li, the school guidance counselor "Hi, Chet, I am so glad I ran into you. I was going to send you an email to set up a time to talk, perhaps this week?" Ms. Zimmerman asks. But before Mr. Li can answer, they are both surprised by the front office secretary calling her name, "Ms. Zimmerman! Glad I caught you!" "Do you know of any special dismissal arrangements for Landon?" the secretary asks from her desk while covering the phone receiver. "No, I do not. Why?" Ms. Zimmerman asks walking over to the secretary's desk. The secretary explains that Landon and his sister had to go to aftercare today because they were not picked up in car line, and now the person who has come to get them is not on the authorized pickup list. The secretary explains she is trying to reach the parents but so far has been unable to. Mr. Li offers to assist the secretary, and upon looking at the worried look on Ms. Zimmerman's face, he promises to text her when it's all worked out.

The following afternoon Ms. Zimmerman and Mr. Li are in his office discussing Landon's family. Ms. Zimmerman says, "I am so glad you were able to help reach Landon's mother yesterday, thanks again for your text." Mr. Li smiles warmly and says, "No problem, the number that was on file with the mom was a landline that was disconnected, but fortunately Landon's sister remembered her new cell phone number so we reached his mother, and she gave permission for the father's girlfriend to take the kids home. Apparently, both she and the father had agreed they would add her to the authorized list but had forgotten to do so."

Ms. Zimmerman nods her head and replies, "I've been concerned about Landon's behavior which is what I wanted to set up a meeting with you to discuss. Landon's moods alternate between sad and withdrawn to irritated and difficult to control—his outburst are frequent and disruptive to the whole class. Unfortunately, it is also happening in physical education, art, and music. Last week both the music and the art teacher came to me to let me know Landon had been involved in an altercation with another student or was simply refusing to listen. This is even more of a change from just a few months ago—it really seems as if his behavior is deteriorating."

Mr. Li takes a deep breath and leans back in his chair before answering. "Yes, I agree, I've had other teachers come to speak to me about his behavior, and Coach Melendez was in here earlier this week when Landon and another student had gotten into a physical altercation; unfortunately, it isn't the first time. It is a cause for concern. Landon's behavior is most likely a result of finding additional changes taking place to his already upturned home life."

Mr. Li continues, "As I understand it from speaking to his mother, his parents' divorce was final earlier this year; however, when his parents separated his mother went back to work and Landon had to adjust to the loss of his father being in his daily life, as well as his mother having to dedicate time to a job." Ms. Zimmerman nods her head in agreement and adds, "Landon just shared with me that he, his mother, and his siblings moved in with his mother's boyfriend." Mr. Li sighs and replies, "Really? I did not know that . . . but it makes clear since given why the office had trouble reaching the mother on the phone yesterday."

Mr. Li pauses to take a sip of his water before continuing. "Regrettably, it appears there are more changes in store for Landon . . . after talking to his father's girlfriend yesterday while we waited to gain Landon's mother's authorization, she informed me that she and Landon's father just got engaged this week, and she has two kids of her own. Thus it is possible that Landon's most recent behavior problems are a direct reflection of his having been told he is going to be part of a stepfamily."

Ms. Zimmerman sighs deeply as she thinks about Landon having to face even more changes to his home life. Mr. Li says, "And Landon's dad's fiancée also told me that it's likely that they may be moving to accommodate the larger family, and I am not certain if keeping Landon and his siblings in their current school is a priority for them. It is possible that they will be changing schools before the end of the year."

"Wow!" Ms. Zimmerman says stunned, "I am not sure how to respond. Landon is already dealing with so much—and he is so distracted and his behavior so erratic—I hate to think how more change will affect his behavior. I have been reading some articles on the effects of divorce on children's classroom behavior in the hopes to learn strategies to help Landon's behavior. However, if you have suggestions I am open to hearing them." Mr. Li nods and says, "Sounds like you have already been doing your best to be sensitive to Landon's home situation while continuing to hold him accountable to classroom rules and policies. I will send over links to more information on the effects of divorce on children in hopes that it will assist you."

Mr. Li pauses and says pensively, "Divorce is not uncommon; however, no two families are alike and I believe our best course here is to continue to offer guidance and support to the kids. At least the parents are not involved in a custody battle like many I've counseled. I have reached out to his parents, and we've talked on several occasions this year. Please remind Landon he can come and see me anytime that he wants to. I think however, that in light of Landon's recent troubles it may be beneficial to invite the parents in for a meeting, so we can all get on the same page." Ms. Zimmerman agrees, and Mr. Li says he'll contact the parents today.

DISCUSSION QUESTIONS

1. Motivation:

   a. What level of Maslow's hierarchy of needs would you say Landon is operating in? Discuss the challenges he faces and how this impedes his movement to the next need level.

   b. How does knowledge of a student's need level in Maslow's hierarchy help teachers motivate students academically?

   c. Can students at these ages achieve the self-actualization level of Maslow's hierarchy? Taking into consideration what is known about self-actualization, how are children going through significant changes in their environment going to have more difficulty reaching self-actualization?

   d. In what ways, can teachers help students feel a sense of belonging—and connect with their peers—both in their classroom or through extra-curricular activities at the school?

   e. Discuss how a child's self-esteem and confidence are related to his motivation, as well as his academic performance.

   f. Speculate on how Landon's being unable to showcase his special talents and abilities on the *All About Me* poster, or being unable to bring in items to show the class, will affect his motivation for assignments and class projects.

   g. How can Landon's self-efficacy be affected by the fact that he was unable to showcase his special talents and abilities on the *All About Me* poster, or that he was unable to bring in items to show the class.

   h. Speculate on how Landon and his sister's home environment could affect their self-efficacy? How will their self-efficacy impact their learning and achievement?

   i. Discuss how Landon's sudden changes in mood, due to his home environment, may affect his relationships with his peers and weaken his social associations.

j. Identify factors in both Landon and his sister's home environments that may affect or hinder their developing self-regulation? Explain how the constant changes in their environment could obstruct their employing self-regulatory behaviors? Explain the impact that poor self-regulation can have on a students' learning and achievement?

2. Social Development:

   a. Outline the different systems of Bronfenbrenner's ecological theory and how they affect a child's development of social skills and social development.
   b. Which Bronfenbrenner's ecological systems would be most influential in this case?
   c. How can unpredictability in behavior, such as Landon is exhibiting in this case, contribute to his sense of isolation from peers and overall feelings of sadness or rejection?
   d. Discuss the importance of a child having set routines and stability in their home environment. Outline the negative effects to a child's self-concept, self-esteem, and self-confidence when having to deal with constant significant changes.
   e. What signs should teachers look for to help identify students who are experiencing changes in their home environment? Generate ideas that teachers can implement in the classroom to assist students of divorce in terms of their social development.
   f. How can schools implement school-wide programs to support teachers in recognizing and consequently helping their students' social relationships as they endure difficult changes in their home lives?

3. Children of Divorce:

   a. Discuss the impact of divorce on students' attention, academic performance, behavior, and relationships with peers in the classroom.
   b. Identify the factors that may lead to children having more difficulties in adjusting to a parent's divorce or separation. Why is it important for teachers, coaches, and counselors to be able to recognize early signs?
   c. In the case, Landon and his sister seem to be displaying separate coping strategies as is seen in their behavior. What developmental differences may exist with how children handle separation or divorce?
   d. Are there gender differences that affect a child's perception and reactions of separation or divorce?
   e. What can teachers do to create classroom environments that are sensitive to children who live with single or stepparents?

f. Discuss the importance of sensitive and ongoing communication with parents to assist students coping with divorce.

g. Extend this discussion to include other significant changes in a child's environment such as parents' loss of job, parent's chronic illness, parental/caregiver loss, loss of a sibling, loss of a pet, etc., and its effects on classroom behavior and academics.

Part V

CLASSROOM MANAGEMENT

Case 15

The Persistently Disruptive Student

Suggested Theories: Classroom Management, Behaviorism, Positive Behavior Support, and Social Cognitive Theory
Teacher Challenges: Disruptive Students
Student Level: Early Elementary School

Ms. Anderson's first-grade class is sitting on the carpet at the back of the room in a semi-circle while Ms. Anderson is sitting on a stool next to a large bulletin board. For the first ten minutes of the day, the class discusses the class rules. Ms. Anderson wants to ensure that since it is the beginning of the school year all of the students know the rules, as well as the consequences for breaking rules. The first day of school, in addition to the rules that she had created for the class, Ms. Anderson allowed the students to produce some of their own and as a class they decided which ones they should add.

She feels this is the best way to build on the school-wide Positive Behavior Support expectations used at Briarwood Elementary. Today the class is reviewing the rules and coming up with examples of how each rule can be broken. They have gone through rules one and two, when a student raises his hand. "Do you have a question, Evan?" Ms. Anderson asks. The student nods his head. "Good job on raising your hand, you have just demonstrated how not to break rule #2, which is not to speak while another is speaking but to raise your hand until I call on you. Very good Evan! Now, go ahead with your question please," Ms. Anderson says.

"So, if I ran when I got up to get in line, I would be in trouble because of rule #3?" asks Evan. "Yes, that is correct Evan, you would have broken rule #3. Can anyone tell me what this rule is?" asks Ms. Anderson as she points to rule #3 on the large board labeled CLASS RULES in red, bold letters. "It is not to run in the classroom!" Harrison shouts excitedly. "Well, I must be imagining things because I thought I heard an answer, but I have not called on anyone yet!" Ms. Anderson says. "And remember, if you break a rule, the first time is a warning, but after that, you have to move your behavior clip to the next color on our classroom rules chart. We all want to stay on green, class, because then you get to go to the class treasure chest on Fridays to turn in the *Briarwood Bucks* you earn for good behavior in the class." Harrison immediately raises his hand, and Ms. Anderson motions for him to answer the question.

"Now, class can we think of why rule #4 is important?" Ms. Anderson asks. Erin, who watched the teacher remind Harrison about the importance of not talking out of turn, raises her hand and Ms. Anderson motions for her to speak. "Because we should keep our hands and feet to ourselves." "Very good, Erin, I can see you were paying attention when we discussed our rules, because it is very important to respect others and their space. So, we do not touch others without their permission. Just like we do not take things from others without their permission, which is our next rule, rule #5," Ms. Anderson answers.

Before the discussion can continue, Ms. Anderson walks over to the side of the classroom where there is an area marked "TIME-OUT," in which Brandon has been sitting because he had been playing at the pencil sharpener, and using it as a time to goof off and distract students who were seated nearby. He was doing this despite being told repeatedly to be working at a center. Ms. Anderson motions for Brandon to join the rest of the class. Brandon immediately tells Ms. Anderson that he knew all of the answers that she asked the class, and then he accuses her of purposely not calling on him even though his hand was raised.

Ms. Anderson explains to Brandon that while in time-out students are not allowed to participate in what the class is doing and they have to move their behavior clip to yellow. She then asks Brandon, "Did you learn anything from being in time-out?" Brandon shakes his head and loudly says, "NO!" "Well that is a shame, Brandon," answers Ms. Anderson as she continues, "because you are not using your indoor voice, and since you tell me that you did not learn how to control yourself better in time-out, you may very well be there again, and miss out on all of the things that the rest of the class has been doing and learning. Now, go sit on the carpet and join your classmates." The class continues to go over the rules before beginning the spelling lesson.

Later that day, the class is cleaning up so that they may line up to go to recess. Ms. Anderson reminds the class that the first tables to go first to recess will be the ones that have put all of their materials away and are sitting in their seats. While the students are putting their materials away, Ms. Anderson notices that Erin and Clarice are pushing each other to try to fit their supplies on the same shelf. Ms. Anderson says, "Now remember class, there is a place for all of the supplies, so there is no need to try to push some other student out of your way in order to get your supplies on a shelf, Erin, Clarice."

Both girls glance over at their teacher and find other places for their supplies before returning to their seats. Soon, Ms. Anderson calls the *"Funky Monkey"* table, and all of the students happily get up and begin to form the line by the door to the playground. "Alright, now the *Purple Squirrels* table may get up and go get in line. Please remember to walk children, not run, or you will be sitting back down," Ms. Anderson warns. All of the students belonging to the *Purple Squirrels* table follow the teacher's instructions, except for Brandon who runs to get in line and knocks Stacey down.

"Brandon, please come here. The rest of the tables, please line up, and then line leader please take the line out to recess." The line leader, Manuel, smiles at Ms. Anderson and begins to walk out of the class, with the rest of his classmates following behind.

"Now, Brandon, you deliberately disobeyed me when I said to walk to get in line. This is the fourth time today you have broken one of the class rules. I am sending a note home to your parents about your behavior. If you misbehave again today, you will not be going to the *treasure chest* on Friday. Because you are now on red, and if you remain on red till the end of the day, you lose the opportunity to turn in your *Briarwood Bucks* for fun prizes in the class treasure chest. Now, go and move your clip to red and sit down until I call you. Since you made the decision to run and push to line-up, you will be last in line today," Ms. Anderson says sternly.

Near the end of the day, the class is working on their reading lessons. The class is divided into three reading groups that differ in ability. While Ms. Anderson is working with one group, her parent volunteer Kona is working with another group, and the third group is working independently. Ms. Anderson's group is taking turns reading aloud. While Harrison is reading, Ms. Anderson notices that a problem is beginning in the group that is working with Kona. In order to prevent the situation from escalating, Ms. Anderson asks Harrison to continue reading and instructs for the rest of the group to follow in the order they have been reading until she returns.

"What is going on?" Ms. Anderson asks Kona. "Well, Ms. Anderson, Brandon just marked all over Evan's paper and when I explained to him that he should apologize, Brandon took the paper and ripped it in half," explains Kona, holding up Evan's torn paper. Evan is visibly upset and explains to Ms. Anderson that Brandon tore his summary of the story they have been reading. "Brandon, what do you have to say?" Ms. Anderson asks. "I was just trying to see it, and he did not let me. It isn't my fault, he just wanted to get me in trouble," Brandon replies angrily.

"Why did you need to see his summary?" Ms. Anderson asks, giving Brandon a chance to explain while she looks at the reading group that she was working with and nods for them to go on reading and quickly glances at the group that is independently working. "Because," replies Brandon. "Because of . . .?" Ms. Anderson asks. "You did not need to be looking at anyone else's summary. You needed to be creating your own, which I see that you did not do," Ms. Anderson says, holding Brandon's paper.

She continues, "I told you earlier that you would be losing a chance to go to the *treasure chest* tomorrow if you misbehaved again and remained on red, so tomorrow you will not be going. Now, please get back to work." Ms. Anderson returns to the reading group that she had been working with.

At the end of the day, Kona and Ms. Anderson are talking while they put supplies away. "Wow, Ms. Anderson, you are really good, I mean you always know what is happening in the room, and sometimes it doesn't even look like you could have seen it. Like when Brandon messed up Jerome's clock project," Kona exclaims. "Thanks for the compliment, I guess I do stay on top of what is going on. I just believe that you can make a difference in all of your students' lives; it is just that with some it is more difficult than with others." Both ladies look at each other and say "Brandon!" in unison.

"Well, he is difficult, but so far I have noticed he has his good days and he has his bad days. I am hoping that a letter home to his folks may help with his behavior. I am not sure the time-out had any effect on his disruptive behavior. Generally, I think the school-wide Positive Behavior Support system is so effective for most students. I really like the consistent message kids get about appropriate behavior, whether from staff in the cafeteria, media center, or even from the patrols in the hallway.

"But some, like Brandon, just need extra effort. Otherwise, I will have to call his parents in for a conference, and we will go from there. One way or another, we will help Brandon to make better choices in the classroom," Ms. Anderson says.

DISCUSSION QUESTIONS

1. Classroom Management:
    a. Relate whether or not Ms. Anderson demonstrates "withitness" in the classroom. Support your answers from the case and if she is not demonstrating "withitness," devise ways that Ms. Anderson could employ.
    b. Outline how Ms. Anderson uses different techniques in the class to deal with discipline problems. Determine their effectiveness.
    c. How effective is time-out as a strategy for reducing misbehavior in the classroom? If used, what are important criteria for using time-out most effectively?

    d. Justify whether you would classify Ms. Anderson's management strategy as a minor or a moderate intervention. Support your answer with examples from the case study.

    e. With regard to the physical makeup of the classroom, conclude the type of arrangement style that Ms. Anderson has in her classroom. Evaluate its effectiveness with regard to classroom management.

    f. Discuss the importance of creating a "community" in the classroom. How does Ms. Anderson accomplish that?

    g. Explain the importance of having clear, concise rules and ensuring that students understand such rules. Refer to case.

    h. Summarize which classroom management models seem most appropriate for use with first-grade students.

    i. Determine which type of Baumrind's classroom management styles Ms. Anderson demonstrates. Rate its effectiveness.

2. Behaviorism:

    a. From the perspective of operant conditioning, differentiate among the different types of reinforcement Ms. Anderson is using.

    b. Illustrate the types of punishments that Ms. Anderson is using.

    c. Judge whether Ms. Anderson is using reinforcement/punishment effectively. Discuss the importance of using reinforcers/punishers effectively to manage student behaviors. Were there any missed opportunities where the teacher left misbehavior unaddressed?

    d. Generate other Skinnerian behavior modification techniques that are available to teachers in managing their classroom.

    e. From the perspective of behaviorism, compare and contrast the advantages and disadvantages of using applied behavioral analyses as a means for managing behavior in the classroom?

    f. What are "logical consequences"? Do you see any instance where the teacher uses logical consequences in her responding to misbehavior? Do you see additional instances where it might have been effectively employed?

    g. What is Positive Behavior Support (PBS) or Positive Behavioral Interventions and Supports (PBIS)? Are school-wide programs effective for improving challenging student behavior?

3. Social Cognitive Theory:

    a. Justify how vicarious reinforcement may be playing a role in this case.

    b. Justify how vicarious punishment may be playing a role in this case.

    c. Determine what role observational learning plays in this case. Design methods for how Ms. Anderson could use observational learning proactively in her class. Generate other techniques that could apply to students' academic learning in different classroom situations.

d. What is teacher efficacy? Do you think Ms. Anderson has high teacher efficacy? How might teacher efficacy impact a teacher's instructional decision making? How might teacher efficacy impact student learning?

4. Communicating with Parents:

a. Do you feel Ms. Anderson is reaching out to Brandon's parents too late? Too early?

b. What recommendations would you make to the teacher as she reaches out to communicate to a parent about their child's misbehavior?

c. What tips for effective parent-teacher conferencing would you offer to Ms. Anderson?

Case 16

Managing Defiant Students

Suggested Theories: Classroom Management, Operant Conditioning, Social
   Cognitive Theory, and Teacher Efficacy
Teacher Challenges: Handling Student Misbehavior, Diminished Instruc-
   tional Time, Effective Reinforcers, Token Economies, and Effective Use
   of Punishments
Student Level: Upper Elementary

Ms. Sanchez's fifth-grade class is coming back from lunch, and as usual they
do not want to settle down and begin their afternoon activities. "Class," Ms.
Sanchez says as she rings the small bell on her desk, "let's get to our desks
and begin our vocabulary lesson without wasting time. Remember, you want
the opportunity to earn *Good Behavior Cash*. We all agreed last week on the
fun rewards and privileges that you can earn with your *Good Behavior Cash*."
Ms. Sanchez points to the board where all the *Good Behavior Cash Prizes* are
listed and the coordinating number of points they are worth.

She hopes that the reminder will help them work toward the goal and
behave since she does believe the children want to earn the *Good Behavior
Cash*. After the teacher's reminder, the students rapidly find their desks, and
Ms. Sanchez exhales in relief to see all the students quietly seated at their
desks working on the synonyms/antonyms section of the vocabulary books as
she instructed. Ms. Sanchez decides to reward a few of the students for following orders, and hands out *Good Behavior Cash*. The students are ecstatic!

Marina and Clara, who are seated next to each other, both show their
excitement for they've both earned enough *Good Behavior Cash* to purchase
rewards they wanted. Ms. Sanchez is so relieved she may have found something that works in getting her students to listen! This is her first year teaching, and she actually had hoped for a position in a younger grade but had been

given fifth grade instead. She is learning many things about this age group from her students, but she feels she isn't always reaching them. Sometimes they accuse her of treating them like babies and other times that she is expecting too much of them. If only she could find a good balance.

With the students quietly working on their vocabulary, Ms. Sanchez calls on Marina, who is assistant teacher for the week, to hand out last night's spelling homework. Assistant teacher is one of the students' favorite privileges to purchase with their *Good Behavior Cash*; however, it is one of the costliest ones, and only students that continuously behave will earn enough *Good Behavior Cash* to purchase it. Ms. Sanchez begins writing sentences on the board that contain the week's vocabulary lesson so they can have a review.

Suddenly, a loud noise startles everyone, and as Ms. Sanchez turns around she sees there is an instant commotion in the back of the room. Students are now standing up, snickering, and pointing toward the back of the room, and Ms. Sanchez is saddened to realize her moment of peace has quickly ended. Ms. Sanchez is filled with apprehension as she makes her way through the sea of students to the back of the room. "What has happened?" Ms. Sanchez asks Tyrese and Srin as she sees them getting up off the floor. Clearly, the boys have fallen out of their chairs—if the chairs turned on their side and the boys being on the floor is any indication.

Upon seeing their teacher standing over them, the boys get up and immediately begin speaking at once. Ms. Sanchez asks them to take turns, so she can hear what occurred. Srin says, "I was just leaning over to reach for my special hat that I got to wear today because it fell off my head and I fell over." Tyrese quickly adds, "I was reaching over to help him get his hat . . . since you are always telling us to do nice things for others, right? Well I tried, but I don't know, I just fell!"

Srin is wearing a hat because that was the reward he chose to purchase with his *Good Behavior Cash*; however, Ms. Sanchez ponders that option now that this is the third problem she's encountered with the wearing of hats. "Now boys, I want the truth!" Ms. Sanchez exclaims in frustration, "Were you boys goofing off?" The boys, now back in their righted seats, do not answer but shake their heads indicating a no. Oh goodness! Again, Ms. Sanchez is confronted with not knowing what to do because she did not see what occurred. Were the boys fighting? Or could it have been a mistake? Could they be telling the truth?

Ms. Sanchez tells the boys to move their pegs down a color on the Behavior Chart. Srin's peg was still on the *green* color, where all students start out each morning—it means *ready to learn*. Thus, Srin gets up and moves his peg to *yellow*, which means *think about your behavior*. Tyrese, on the other hand, had already moved his peg to *yellow* earlier in the day and now he would be moving his peg to *orange*, which means *teacher's choice of consequence*.

Tyrese, unlike Srin, doesn't immediately follow Ms. Sanchez's command to change his color. Instead, he throws his hands in the air and says defiantly, "Oh c'mon, Ms. Sanchez! That isn't fair!"

Ms. Sanchez ignores his outburst and tells him firmly that since he did not move his color, she will move it for him and he's now to go to the *Isolation Station*. The *Isolation Station* consists of a desk in the back corner of the room reserved for students whose behavior is continuously disrupting the class. Tyrese begins to move his things over to the *Isolation Station,* but he does so slowly and uses every attempt to be loud and disruptive, making it impossible for many of the students, particularly the ones seated near him in the room, to listen to the teacher's lesson.

Ms. Sanchez thinks to stop the lesson again so she can move Tyrese's peg down to the last color. However, she sees she has not gotten far in her instruction, and the end of the school day is drawing near.

No sooner is Ms. Sanchez's attention diverted to assist a student that she sees, another behavioral problem is occurring with a few of the girls. Ms. Sanchez knows that many of the students like to draw in their notebooks. It is, in fact, a favorite activity to do in *free choice*—a thirty-minute block of time right before dismissal that Ms. Sanchez has reserved a few times a week for students to choose what they would like to do. However, Ms. Sanchez sees that a few of the girls have chosen to draw during the lesson. She decides to move closer to them in hopes they will quickly put the art away and get back on track.

However, one of the students, Jazmin, is turned completely around in her seat to share her drawing with Alecia, and while Alecia tries to warn Jazmin of the teacher's approach, she doesn't do so in time. "Jazmin," Ms. Sanchez says firmly, "what are you doing turned around in your seat? Why don't you have your vocabulary workbook out?" Ms. Sanchez reaches over and takes her drawing and says, "This is not art class, nor is it *free choice* time, and I see that you did not complete the problems that you were assigned prior to my beginning the lesson. Please move your peg down a color on the behavior board."

Jazmin whines and offers excuses as to why she was drawing, telling the teacher she was taking too much time dealing with Tyrese and she got bored. As always, her students generate various invalid excuses to try to explain their misbehavior.

Since Jazmin peg was already on *yellow*, she is now moving to *orange* which means *teacher's choice of consequence*. Ms. Sanchez says, "Jazmin, during *free choice time*, you will complete all of the work you did not complete today and whatever you don't finish, you will do for homework." Jazmin returns to her desk and says vehemently, "Why are you being so mean? I wasn't doing anything wrong! And why am I the only one getting punished?

Why isn't anyone else who was drawing getting in trouble? And yesterday you caught an entire group of students doodling during science, and you didn't give them a consequence! You like them and not me!"

Ms. Sanchez replies sternly, "You have one chance to sit down, be quiet, and get back to work or I am sending you to the principal's office young lady." Jazmin sits down but is angry and says under her breath, "Funny . . . but isn't the next color we move our dumb peg to next on the idiotic behavior chart *red*? Unless I can't see straight that is *parent contact*, not principal . . . Do you even know your own stupid system or maybe you can't read?" The students around Jazmin giggle, and a few nod their heads indicating that they agree; Jazmin's misbehavior, however, goes unnoticed because it is the end of the day and the class is ready to line up for dismissal.

As usual, her students are not orderly when it comes to transitions and are presently going in all different directions gathering their belongings in a disorganized fashion. Ms. Sanchez thinks, like always, we'll be one of the last classes to arrive at the dismissal area. Classes are walking by the open door of Ms. Sanchez's classroom and she hollers, "Let's get moving kids, we're behind schedule!" Finally, it seems most of the class has gathered their belongings and are in line when Ms. Sanchez sees that there are students' projects all over the floor by the door.

"Oh no! Did someone knock into the table by the door, where we always put our projects? The projects for Parent's Week are all over the floor!" Ms. Sanchez exclaims rushing to salvage the work before it is trampled. She hears many students lament and some get out of line to quickly help pick them up. "Who did this? Who was so careless?" Ms. Sanchez asks urgently to no one in particular. No one comes forward until other students who witnessed what happened tell on the students responsible.

Ms. Sanchez reprimands them for their carelessness, their lack of sincerity at admitting their wrongdoing, and their unwillingness to make the situation better by picking up the projects. She assigns them to help clean up the mess, as well as complete an *Apology Report* for homework.

Complaints are heard throughout; however, Erica approaches Ms. Sanchez and says shyly, "I'm sorry Ms. Sanchez, I think I might have hit a few of them with my backpack; but, um, well I don't need to complete an *Apology Report* right? I was on *green* on the behavior chart. So this would move my peg to *yellow*, which is *think about your behavior* not to *orange* where I would have a *consequence*." Ms. Sanchez replies strictly, "No, everyone that was responsible completes an *Apology Report*! So I expect yours tomorrow!"

Ms. Sanchez sees that many of the students helping to clean up were not the ones responsible for the mess, and she decides this is a perfect opportunity to give out *Good Behavior Cash* to reward their thoughtful actions. She realizes as she gives out the *Good Behavior Cash* that she had forgotten to give those out throughout the day, as she intended to do when she started the system. Oh well! I guess I'll just give extra *Good Behavior Cash* right now to the students that are helping and to the ones that have been patiently waiting in line to make up for it!

As always, the students earning the *Good Behavior Cash* are excited and the ones that didn't earn the cash are upset. The class is finally moving to the dismissal area, and as Ms. Sanchez walks by Tyrese, he asks her grumpily, "How come I didn't get any *Good Behavior Cash*?" Alecia, who is a few students behind him, adds, "Yeah, me too!" Ms. Sanchez quickly answers distractedly as she signals for two students in the back to stop fooling around, "Because neither one of you is being quiet in line nor did you help pick up the projects."

Alecia crosses her arms across her chest and replies whining, "But . . . but . . . you never see us when we are doing anything good, Ms. Sanchez! When we are doing good things you don't give out the *Good Behavior Cash!* We're never gonna get enough to buy any good rewards!" Tyrese and a few other students shout out in agreement. Ms. Sanchez ignores the complaints and instead announces to the class that since the majority of the class has not been quiet or well-behaved walking in line, tomorrow instead of *free choice time*, the class is going to practice walking in line properly. The groans of her students only increase upon hearing the news.

The following day, Ms. Sanchez's students are turning in homework and lining up for music. Ms. Sanchez hopes that they can get out to music on time today, because the music teacher told her last week that her students were behind in being prepared for the Spring concert due to their always being late getting to her.

Ms. Sanchez reminds them of the class incentive for a reward. "Remember everyone, you all want to earn compliments from other adults at the school for good behavior while walking in line. Remember the class will get two tickets if the compliment is coming from another teacher or staff member, three tickets if it is a parent volunteer or school administrator—like guidance counselor, and five tickets if we can get one from the principal! And remember if you all get an excellent in behavior in art, or PE, or . . . ahem, ahem music, which we're going to right now, that will earn you seven tickets toward the class goal you chose of a movie and popcorn party!"

Several students show their excitement; however, a few of the well-behaved students express their doubts to Ms. Sanchez as she walks by. "Do you really think we can get everyone to behave in line?" asks Clara. "Yeah Ms. Sanchez, do you think so? And in music and art too?" asks Srin. Ms. Sanchez is about to respond when Marina says, "I don't know. . . . We still have a lot of tickets to go to get to the goal. So many other classes have gotten to their class goals a few times already." Ms. Sanchez is about to impart encouraging words to motivate them when a difficulty ensues in the front of the line that she must handle before it escalates.

Ms. Sanchez can hear Parker and Declan arguing as she approaches, and frankly she cannot believe that those two students are arguing again; she just had a stern talk with them yesterday about their behavior in lunch. They were in line at the cafeteria to buy lunch and Declan's lunch tray had gotten knocked over. Parker said it was an accident, but Declan said Parker had done it intentionally. Since the lunch monitor had not seen the incident, he asked both boys to help clean it up and informed her of what happened.

Ms. Sanchez had both boys sit in the *Isolation Station* upon returning from lunch and assigned them an *Apology Report* for homework, even though both boys' pegs were on green at that time. An *Apology Report* is a form in which the student is asked to think on the misbehavior and write how they can improve themselves for next time. Ms. Sanchez requires that parents sign the report and bring it back the following day. Parker had completed it, and had his parents sign it, but Declan had not.

In fact, Declan's mom had written an email letting her know that her son would not be completing the report for she did not believe he had been at fault at lunch. She asked for proof that he had been responsible and wanted to meet with her, since she felt that this was not the first time Ms. Sanchez had wrongly accused Declan. Ms. Sanchez was taken aback at the parent's response; after all, wasn't she the teacher? Why would a parent think to question her methods?

"Parker! Declan! Stop shouting! You are not using inside voices!" Ms. Sanchez says exasperatedly. The boys ignore the teacher's request. "Parker, stop saying I suck at sports! Take it back! I am a million times better that you! You run like a little baby! You spend more time on the ground than playing," Declan says intensely. "Shut up Declan, or I'm going to punch you in the face!" Parker yells, reaching over to Declan. Ms. Sanchez is alarmed and jumps in front of Parker, interceding his getting to Declan, "Whoa! Stop that right this minute, Parker! You cannot threaten other students or hit them!"

Parker looks at her defiantly and shouts, "He started it! He called me names in recess today, but you don't hear him! You don't hear anything! Ask everyone, they know! He is a total jerk, and I'm sick of him making fun of me and getting others to do the same!" Declan shakes his head and says, "No way Ms. Sanchez, I did not call him a name, and I am not picking on him at all! He's the one that knocked my lunch down yesterday remember? He did that because he was mad that he never beats me at anything! It's not our fault he can't keep up when we play sports in recess! And now he likes Marina and she likes me! He's just jealous! Ask the class!"

Ms. Sanchez exhales in silent frustration because once again she finds herself in a situation where she truly is unsure who is telling the truth or what exactly has happened. She never got the impression that Parker and Declan were the best of friends, but aside from the incident at lunch, she hadn't noticed them actually disliking each other. Had she really overlooked a problem that has been ongoing with these students? A problem that has spiraled into verbal and physical aggression? "Boys, this is not acceptable! Since you all cannot play sports fairly or nicely at recess, there are no more sports allowed to be played at recess.

All the boys in the class will have to find other activities to partake in. In addition, both of you have lost the privilege of walking in line with your friends, until further notice you will walk next to me." Ms. Sanchez walks back to the end of the line with the two boys unhappily behind her. "But, . . . but for how long can't we play sports? What about the rest of us that have not gotten in trouble playing sports at recess? Why can't we play?" Srin asks. "Because I said so. It's a class punishment for at least a week. I don't want to hear any more about it," Ms. Sanchez answers firmly.

A few students remark how they're late for music again and that with all the fighting they aren't going to get any compliments; regrettably, she has to agree with them. She feels that despite her best intentions, all these interruptions are always delaying them. However, what more can she do? She fears this is not the end of this problem between Parker and Declan, and she has to speak to the principal due to the nature of their altercation; and if Declan's mother's response to the *Apology Report* is any indication, it is likely she will not be happy to hear of today's incident.

Later that day, Ms. Sanchez brings out the *Good Behavior Cash* and begins awarding in hopes that the students will settle down and finish the short stories they began the day before. Ms. Sanchez hopes that there will be enough time for all the students to complete the assignment without problems because they are running behind schedule today, and she prefers not to take time away from the math lesson again. However, just as Ms. Sanchez thinks the class is doing well, two students begin to argue.

Although she tries to intercede, in the end she has to have one student change his color and complete an *Apology Report* for homework, while the other student goes to sit in the *Isolation Station* in order to end the argument. The day unfortunately continues to prove difficult for Ms. Sanchez, when later that day during social studies, she checks her students' group progress on their Civil War timelines and discovers some groups are behind schedule.

Ms. Sanchez is concerned that some student groups seemed to have misunderstood portions of the assignment and hopes that all the time she has spent on classroom misbehaviors has not affected the students' work too terribly, because she's unsure of how to make up for the time lost. Ms. Sanchez has been consistently assigning extra work every week for homework that was not completed in class, which adds to the students' regular homework. She would consider sending home the social studies assignment but fears she'll receive a ton of parent complaints that frankly she does not have time to address.

She hopes the assistance she provides today to the groups that have fallen behind is enough; if not, she presumes she'll have to add a curve to the grades again to account for the errors in understanding.

"Now remember class," Ms. Sanchez says as she walks over to the groups using the computers for their research, "use your time wisely on the computers so that you can add creativity to your timelines—remember though, time is limited!" Ms. Sanchez has come to stand over Tyrese's group and hears Jazmin say, "Stop making marks all over my paper Tyrese! These are my social studies notes and I don't want them ruined!" Jazmin exclaims, annoyed and looks over to Ms. Sanchez for help. Ms. Sanchez asks Tyrese to help erase the marks on Jazmin's paper and get back to work.

However, Parker, who is also in this group says, "Ms. Sanchez, it's not fair that we now can't get on the computer today to research because you banned our group from computer use all week! It was only Tyrese that was playing games online and not working! And look! He's not even helping us!" Ms. Sanchez looks closer at Tyrese's desk and sees that while he has a folder on his desk, it doesn't contain social studies work in it; instead it looks like just loose-leaf papers.

Ms. Sanchez picks up a few of the papers in Tyrese's folder including one he was deliberately trying to hide under the rest, "Tyrese, while I see that this drawing of a girl is quite nice, you need to put it away right now along with this other creation you have made here because none of this is for social studies." Ms. Sanchez says pointing to the broken pen that he has attached to another broken pen with tape; evidence that he is inappropriately using his school supplies and from the looks of the odd creation has been off-task for quite some time. "But, um, Jazmin was drawing yesterday and you didn't tell her anything!" Tyrese protests.

"Well, that was different, now don't argue with me or you'll move the behavior peg again today," replies Ms. Sanchez strictly before adding, "And where are your social studies notes? How are you contributing to your group's timeline without them?" Tyrese looks flustered but before he can reply, Jazmin interjects, "That's because he isn't doing any work, like Parker said. He is only drawing pictures of Clara because he really, really likes her! He's got a crush on her! Don't you Tyrese?" Jazmin asks smugly.

Then Parker adds, "Uh huh, he does! But he can't help us on this timeline because he hasn't done the homework. Go ahead Tyrese, name one thing that happened after the Civil War. Oh you can't? But . . . you can tell us all about Clara." The other students in the group agree, and the room begins to fill with students' whispers and snickers. Tyrese's face turns red showing his embarrassment; he crumples up the drawing, throwing it toward the trash and kicks his chair over shouting, "Shut up you morons! I hate you! All of you!"

Before Ms. Sanchez has a chance to respond, Tyrese runs toward the back door of the classroom and walks out, yelling obscenities. Ms. Sanchez is flustered and hopes the students do not notice. She tries to remain calm, as she knows the students are watching the situation carefully. She walks calmly over to the intercom and calls the assistant principal—when he answers, she alerts him of the occurrence. Ms. Sanchez then asks Marina, her teacher's helper this week, to watch the class. "Marina, write the names of the students who misbehave on the board, while I see where Tyrese has gone." Marina nods as she goes over to stand by the whiteboard.

As the end of the week comes to a close, Ms. Sanchez reflects on her experiences with her students over the course of the past month. She feels she's had more than her share of difficult moments, and upon thinking about them she isn't sure how she would have handled them differently. She had difficulties that ended with several students going to the principal—Tyrese's situation was the worst with his leaving the class. Fortunately, he had not gone far; however, the principal called his parents in for a meeting that same afternoon to discuss his behavior and the steps that would be taken to assure it would not be repeated.

Declan and Parker's problems had also led them to the principal; however, Declan's mother had not been deterred in declaring her methods unjust and accused Ms. Sanchez of not being able to provide proof that it had been Declan who had been at fault for any of the altercations. In fact, she claimed that Declan was the target of the other child's attacks—a point that the principal seemed to agree with after hearing about all the incidents. Other parents had also sent emails and called for meetings, as they felt was unfairly punishing the entire class for the actions of a few of the students.

Additionally, they wanted to know why their students hadn't earned any of the whole-class rewards they had been told they were working toward, while other fifth-grade classes had. Ms. Sanchez feels as though no matter what technique she tries to implement; it doesn't appear to work or it doesn't work for long. What is she doing wrong she wonders? She sees other fellow teachers and they all seem to be in control. They don't seem to be encountering this many problems. She is tired of all these problems. Is it possible, she wonders, that has chosen the wrong career path?

DISCUSSION QUESTIONS

1. Classroom Management:
    a. Relate whether or not Ms. Sanchez demonstrates "withitness" in the classroom. Support your answers from the case and if she is not demonstrating "withitness," devise ways that this teacher could employ to become more "withit."

b. Outline how Ms. Sanchez uses different techniques in the class to deal with discipline problems. Determine their effectiveness.

c. How effective is the *Isolation Station* for reducing misbehavior in the classroom? What is its intended purpose and what important criteria should be used when isolating students for misbehaving?

d. Justify whether you would classify Ms. Sanchez's management strategy as a minor or a moderate intervention. Support your answer with examples from the case study.

e. With regard to the physical makeup of the classroom, conclude the type(s) of arrangement style that Ms. Sanchez has in her classroom. Evaluate its effectiveness with regard to classroom management.

f. Discuss the importance of creating a "community" in the classroom. Is Ms. Sanchez creating that sense of community in the classroom? How are the classroom management problems this teacher is encountering affecting student morale in the class?

g. Explain the importance of having clear, concise rules and ensuring that students understand such rules. What problems can you identify that the teacher in the case is having with the rules of her classroom?

h. Discuss ways that teachers can handle students who constantly make excuses for behavior. How can teachers help to make them more accountable for their actions?

i. Summarize which classroom management models seem most appropriate for use with fourth-grade students.

j. Determine which type of Baumrind's classroom management styles Ms. Sanchez demonstrates. Use examples from the case and rate its effectiveness.

k. Speculate on how the teacher's classroom management style is interfering with her instructional time, instructional goals, and her students' learning.

2. Behaviorism:

a. From the perspective of operant conditioning, differentiate among the different types of reinforcement Ms. Sanchez is using. Judge their effectiveness.

b. Illustrate the types of punishments that Ms. Sanchez is using. Judge their effectiveness.

c. Identify the token economy used in this case. Is it an effective method for controlling behavior in the class? Why or why not? What struggles are students citing for reaching the most expensive rewards?

d. Discuss how teachers should handle severe misbehavior such as we see in this case. How did this teacher's use of reinforcers/punishers contribute to students' continuous misbehavior? Is the teacher giving the students an equal chance at earning reinforcement?

    e. Outline the challenges that students in this class face with regard to obtaining the group rewards.

    f. Generate other Skinnerian behavior modification techniques that are available to teachers in managing their classroom.

    g. From the perspective of behaviorism, compare and contrast the advantages and disadvantages of using applied behavioral analyses as a means for managing behavior in the classroom?

    h. Identify the concept of a "logical consequence." Choose instances in the case where the teacher uses logical consequences in her responding to misbehavior. Are these consequences working effectively for this teacher? Do you see additional instances where it might have been effectively employed?

    i. What is Positive Behavior Support (PBS) or Positive Behavioral Interventions and Supports (PBIS)? Are school-wide programs effective for improving challenging student behavior?

3. Social Cognitive Theory:

    a. Justify how vicarious reinforcement may be playing a role in this case.

    b. Justify how vicarious punishment may be playing a role in this case.

    c. Determine what role observational learning plays in this case. Design methods for how Ms. Sanchez could use observational learning proactively in her class. Generate other techniques that could apply to students' academic learning in different classroom situations.

    d. Outline examples from the case in which the students are learning via response facilitation. Do you believe these examples to be positive ones? How can this teacher use inhibition/disinhibition in his class to help student's behavior?

    e. What is teacher efficacy? Distinguish between personal and general teaching efficacy. Do you think Ms. Sanchez has high or low personal teacher efficacy? Do you think Ms. Sanchez has high or low general teacher efficacy? How is this demonstrated in the case?

    f. How has Ms. Sanchez's teacher efficacy impacted her instructional decision making and classroom management choices? How might Ms. Sanchez's teacher efficacy impact her students' learning? How is this demonstrated in the case?

Part VI

INSTRUCTIONAL APPROACHES

Case 17

Balanced Instruction

Mindful Use of Technology

Suggested Theories: Teacher-Centered Instruction, Direct Instruction, Expository Learning & Assessment, Positive Learning Environments, Technology and Education

Teacher Challenges: Using Technology Effectively in the Classroom; Safe Internet Use; Creating Effective Project-Based Learning Opportunities; Creating Productive Learning Environments, SES Barriers & Technology Skills

Grade Level: Upper Elementary

Jennifer Schwarz is seated in the back of her classroom surrounded by all her fifth-graders, who are seated on the floor on the carpet. Mrs. Schwarz is instructing her students on a new multimedia project that she is assigning to the class and making sure that the students do not have any last minute questions.

She has already explained the project itself earlier in the week, as well as reminded her students to tell their parents that the project requires they complete portions of it at home. Although the multimedia project is building on information that the students have already acquired, Mrs. Schwarz knows that the majority of the students have never completed this type of assignment before. Thus, she wants to ensure they have a strong knowledge of the concepts included in the project prior to the students getting started.

Mrs. Schwarz has decided that for the lessons that relate to the project, she is going to instruct her students explicitly to ensure that students don't miss important information. She then begins instructing them using carefully articulated lessons, where she has broken down the cognitive skills needed to complete the assignment into small units. Mrs. Schwarz is careful to provide clear explanations, descriptions, and examples in sequence. She confirms that her students are understanding her directions by asking them to respond with a show of hands.

Mrs. Schwarz then provides students with a few opportunities for guided practice on the concepts just learned and offers assistance to those students whom she sees may be lacking mastery. Finally, Mrs. Schwarz offers the students a recap of the lesson and concludes by having the students return to their seats and begin independently working on the first portion of the assignment. She will collect this portion of the assignment and assess it for understanding, before allowing students to complete the remaining parts of the assignment on their own and earn a grade.

It is soon time to line up for lunch, and Mrs. Schwarz asks the students to turn in their assignments before getting in line. As the students are turning in their work, Mrs. Schwarz says, "Now remember class, we discussed how you will be using the internet to complete this project? Okay so, I have put an *Internet Safety Handbook* in each of your cubbies this morning. It's the handbook we went over yesterday. Remember how we discussed important information about when you are online? The office has printed a handbook out for each of you."

"Please take it home, read it with your parents, and ask them to sign the last page before you return it to me. I will need to have the signed page before I allow you to use the computers here in the classroom for your project." Mrs. Schwarz's students have all lined up, and she sees Camryn has her hand up. "Yes, Camryn," Mrs. Schwarz says. "Can we use videos or podcasts?" Camryn asks. "Sure, as long as they are appropriately related to your topic," Mrs. Schwarz answers and calls on another student whose hand is raised. "Hmm, do we have to use all educational sites? You know like National Geographic Kids or can we use blogs and webpages we find that are on our topic?"

Mrs. Schwarz considers Brady's question and says thoughtfully, "Well as long as you can verify that it is not just someone's opinion on the subject. For example, if we as a class create a blog would all the information we put on that blog be factual?" Students raise their hands to answer and the consensus is that it would not all be facts. Mrs. Schwarz agrees and reminds the students of the class discussion they had about the correct websites to search and the importance of making sure that information gathered on the internet be accurate when used for any classroom project or assignment.

At the end of the week, Mrs. Schwarz stops by the gym where she likes to enjoy her workouts after the school day has finished. After her workout, she stops by the gym's eatery to enjoy a post-workout beverage. She is happily thinking about how well most of her students did on the first portion of the multimedia assignment that they completed after her lesson. She is also getting many of the signed handbook pages back and students have been working on the next phase of the project all week long.

Her thoughts are interrupted when she sees an old colleague, Enrique Menendez, whom she taught with before getting her present teaching position. Jennifer calls out to Enrique and invites him to share her table overlooking a peaceful water fountain. The two greet each other warmly and Enrique says, "Well, video chatting and email has definitely served us well, but it's so nice to run into you face-to-face." Jennifer agrees as they catch up on their families and an upcoming 5K run that they have both signed up to do.

"So, how's it going with your students? All is still good?" Enrique asks. "Yes, the students are wonderful, very eager to learn. I am certainly glad that I have stayed with this age group since I had developed some neat ideas and projects that now I can continue to use at this school. So all that hard work did not go to waste!" Jennifer says. Enrique replies, "Absolutely. And that project you were telling me about with all the technology, did you assign it yet? As you were describing it to me I thought it sounded fantastic, but I would have worried that I'd encounter difficulties with students' technology skills. But maybe your students are more advanced?"

Jennifer takes a drink of her beverage and says, "I assigned it earlier this week. You know, I was just thinking that it was all going very well . . . but now that you ask, I realize that there have been some challenges. To answer your question, some of my students are very technologically advanced; seems they have owned tablets and computers for the better part of their lives. So, for them, any assignment requiring technology is not difficult. However, there are students whose skills are lacking, in particular those students that are bused in to the school. As I work with them it is becoming very apparent that they don't always have access to technology at home, and so anything requiring technology will be a struggle for them. Especially since we are required to assign online tutorials and these students rarely complete them." Enrique seems puzzled and asks, "What tutorials? I don't think I am familiar with those?"

Jennifer replies enthusiastically, "Oh! They're online educational programs that the school has purchased licenses for. They're outstanding! I like to assign them as homework for students to practice skills learned in class. And I feel the best part is when the student completes them, the system sends the teacher a completed report. The report lets you know which students completed the work and also at which level, so you can keep track of each student's performance level. The system also adjusts instruction to the students' level, making the entire program tailored to each student's ability."

Enrique replies nodding, "Oh yes, I have heard of those! Wow! I'm glad to hear that they work! However, what happens to those students you were just talking about that do not have internet at home and then don't complete them? Are you required to hold them accountable in some way?"

Jennifer's cell phone rings and she silences it before answering, "The students that stay in aftercare get a chance to complete them since they have access to the computers for assignments. The students that have come to me letting me know they cannot complete them at home and aren't in aftercare I give them similar assignments on paper. Thus, while they aren't falling behind academically, their continued lack of exposure to technology is a concern."

Enrique considers what Jennifer is saying and leans back in his chair. "Yes, that is certainly true. You know, I think about that quite a bit because as I have commented to you, our problems with lack of funding in my school continue. We have little technology available to us, and so my students will certainly not acquire much proficiency in technology; not to mention that the software available in school districts with greater funding is not likely to be available to those of us who teach in the low socioeconomic areas." Jennifer agrees these issues are concerning, especially when you consider the increasing role that technology will play in the future.

Jennifer and Enrique continue to talk and move to some of the more similar concerns they face. "It is crazy how students will forget to bring in assignments all the time!" Jennifer says and exhales before continuing, "Some of my students have yet to return their signed technology safety handbook page, even though they know that without it they can't get on the internet at school. It's frustrating that some of them are the same students who do not have access to the internet at home so you'd think they would remember!"

Enrique laughs and says, "Well, I don't think that we are going to see a decline in that anytime soon! Something I would like to see a decline in is parent complaints." Jennifer replies quickly, "Oh, me too. It seems that I spend a lot of time returning emails and calls from parents who are constantly asking for more time on school work or wanting me to excuse their kids from make-up work."

Enrique looks puzzled and says, "Really? You have kids that are out a lot?" Jennifer sighs and says, "Yes, but they're not sick. They take vacations during school and will argue that it's for family events, or are involved in competitive sports travel leagues that require they are away for games—hence the need for make-up work. I also have many students that are involved in a large number of afterschool activities, and it often competes with their ability to complete regular homework, let alone projects."

"Like with this project I just assigned," she continues, "I have already received quite a few emails and phone calls from parents letting me know that they were going to need an extension on the project's due date, telling me their children have upcoming extracurricular commitments such as recitals, tournaments, sports, competitions, etc., that would make it impossible for the students to complete their work on time . . . but as I add more time to this project's due date, I feel that now it may be compromising the children's learning of the unit the project is based on." Enrique commiserates with her as the two teachers continue to converse a while longer before wishing each other a good weekend and leaving to go home for the day.

As the following week arrives, Mrs. Schwarz continues to give class time for the students to resume work on their multimedia projects in class. The students that returned their signed handbook pages are working on the computers, while the rest are working on other aspects of their project. "Camryn, what is that you are typing on that webpage?" Mrs. Schwarz asks, as she reaches the student's computer station. "This website is asking for my email address before it gives me information . . . so I was going to give my parents' email," Camryn replies offhandedly.

"No, Camryn, do not do that. Remember what we discussed about personal information? You do not give it out to anyone who asks you for it on the internet unless you check with either me when you are in school or your parents when you are at home," Mrs. Schwarz answers. Camryn suddenly appears concerned and says, "Am I in trouble? I mean, I thought you meant personal things like your address and last name and stuff, but not actually emails. Sorry." Mrs. Schwarz answers sympathetically, "No, you aren't in trouble; however, I do want all of you to listen carefully to all the things we have discussed with regard to internet safety Okay?"

Camryn nods as do other students listening to the exchange. It is clear to Mrs. Schwarz that she will need to constantly remind and monitor students while they are online in the classroom, because they are not always following her online safety instructions. Yesterday she intervened as a student attempted to turn on the computer's camera to allow a site to capture their image while another student had started clicking on ads that appeared and redirected them to other sites. She wonders if she should create a poster as a visual reminder for online safety and attach it to the wall above the computers. Maybe, it will help to have the rules right in front of them.

Mrs. Schwartz walks over to answer a student's question and finds herself once again helping the same students that she has been helping since the project was assigned. She had intended this assignment to be one in which after she explained the project and taught the skills, the students would be able to create the project with little guidance thereby showcasing their independent abilities. However, she has found that while some students are certainly able to accomplish the task as intended, others are requiring much more direction than she believes is necessary at this age.

Some have come to her frustrated because they want more structure for how to do the project and then want constant reassurance that they're on the right track. Other students, like she had discussed with Enrique, lack technological skills and her consistently helping them is taking too much time away from the class's instructional time. Especially when some students are so far behind the rest, she finds herself directing them step-by-step on inserting the media into their project. When students are lacking the necessary technological skills to complete the project, then how much are they actually profiting from this project she wonders?

Finally, there have been some disgruntled parents that feel that she is requiring too much technological proficiency from the students. They feel a sense of inadequacy at not being able to assist their children because they aren't that skillful in technology. She realizes that the completed projects are going to exhibit a much wider range of results than she had anticipated. This has led her to wonder how each student's learning of the unit will be related to their success or lack thereof in completing the project.

It is the end of the week, and the students are having a lesson in science. Mrs. Schwarz explains how that day's information is a continuation of what they have been learning all week, and this new unit is connected to what they have been learning all week on the physical properties of matter. She indicates on the screen where the lesson is projected, that she has highlighted portions in the lesson she feels are important for them to learn and wants it written in their notebooks. She also reminds them to pay attention to bold face words as they too signal importance.

"Okay everyone, I'm going to start our interactive flash cards. When I click on the card and the question appears I will call on someone to give me the answer. Here we go," Mrs. Schwarz says as she clicks on the card and she proceeds to read out loud, "Who can tell me how many forms matter can exist in?" Mrs. Schwarz calls on Jake whose hand is raised. "Three," Jake replies. Mrs. Schwarz tells him that is correct and moves to the next question that appears, asking "And what are the forms?" and then calling on Raquel. "Liquid, gas, and solid," Raquel says.

"Great job you two!" Mrs. Schwarz exclaims and continues the lesson calling on other students. Some students grapple with a correct response, and Mrs. Schwarz proceeds to give them a small hint to consider as they search for a correct response. After a few seconds, if the student cannot give the right answer, then she asks another student. Mrs. Schwarz makes certain that by the end of the lesson, the majority of her students have had a chance to give an example and demonstrate to her they can apply what they have learned.

After recess the students continue the new grammar unit they began on Monday on diagramming sentences for which Mrs. Schwarz uses the interactive whiteboard, a technology program that allows students to actively work with the lesson that is projected on the screen. Various sentences are displayed on her computer, which are then projected onto the large screen in front of the class. When the student is called up to go to the whiteboard, they will get to correct the sentence right on the screen by using the special pen.

If the student corrects the sentence accurately, there will be a reward in the form of an animated character dancing and fireworks that shoot off on the screen. The students really enjoy the funny characters as well as the recognition. On the other hand, if the student is unable to correct the sentence, the program will give them subsequent chances to accurately correct the sentence while an animated character will say messages like "Oops, that's not right," or "Try again, you can do it!" Mrs. Schwarz is a fan of this software, as she feels it allows her students to view errors as a part of learning.

Mrs. Schwarz usually finishes the lesson with a review of what was learned and incorporates short video clips into the review. The videos she uses depict students doing problems similar to the ones that the class just completed. She likes to show video clips where the students are correctly identifying grammar errors in sentences and correcting them. The last video clip contains what Mrs. Schwarz calls a *Hot Problem* and it consists of a short paragraph filled with errors that are more challenging and thought-provoking than the ones they have just worked on.

Mrs. Schwarz times the students to see how many errors they can identify and write down on their papers before the designated time is up. Mrs. Schwarz then shows them the corrected sentences and reviews each error; she finds that students really enjoy this exercise and look forward to it. Mrs. Schwarz feels that her students learn not only from the errors they did correctly recognize but also from the ones they weren't able to catch in the exercise. She uses similar interactive software in math, science, and social studies.

Later that day during her planning period, Mrs. Schwarz is looking over her students' grades across all subjects in order to determine which students she may need to request a parent conference with when progress reports go out to parents. In looking over her students' grades, she has been noticing patterns that have concerned her. It appears that students' grades have not increased across all subjects as a result of her infusing more technology into her instruction; in fact, as compared to last quarter, some students have shown a significant decline in their grades in some of the subjects.

Upon closer inspection, Mrs. Schwarz discovers that many of the students have not only performed poorer on in-class assignments on those subjects this quarter but that their online tutorial progress is also showing students are wrestling with many of the concepts. The tutorial results convey that students are doing a greater number of questions to reach the same goal than they did last quarter and also that it is taking them more time to complete a section. While certainly some of it could be due to the nature of the material being taught this quarter, she can't help but think that's not the only reason.

Could it be that some of the more innovative technology-infused instruction may not work as effectively across the board for all the subjects? In fact, the subjects that students' grades seem to be most affected this quarter are the ones that she decreased her formal instruction methods in favor of the more innovative technology uses. So, should she reduce the use of technology she wonders? Or maybe use the technology from this tutorial to inform her teaching? How is she to balance out her students' instruction to provide them with the necessary skills while also incorporating the latest technology?

DISCUSSION QUESTIONS

1. Teacher-Centered Instruction:

   a. Discuss the planning methods when preparing teacher-centered instruction.
   b. Explain approaches characteristically associated with teacher-centered instruction. Identify the characteristics of teacher-centered instruction used in this case.
   c. Which instructional method is the teacher in the case study using at the beginning of the case? Describe its effectiveness with regard to her goal for the instruction.
   d. What other teacher-centered instructional approaches is the teacher in this case using? Is she effective in using this type of instruction?
   e. Outline the potential benefits of using teacher-centered instruction. Diagram what techniques increase the effectiveness of teacher-centered instruction.
   f. Summarize how wait-time with regard to questioning affects student learning. Describe how the teacher in the case study uses questioning. Does she use it effectively? Why or why not?
   g. What elements of teacher-centered instruction and student-centered instruction do you see in this case? Cite examples from the case. Do you feel the teacher has created a proper balance between teacher and student-centered instruction?
   h. The teacher in the case thinks about some of the patterns that she sees emerging in the students' grades. Do you feel this pattern is linked to her instructional methods? Why or why not? Discuss the importance of identifying the most effective instructional strategy for your students.
   i. Do you feel this teacher has created a productive classroom climate? Why or why not? Do you feel she has adequate classroom organization?
   j. Do you think Mrs. Schwarz attempts to organize lessons so they are effectively sequenced and build on one another? Why is this important?

k. What are advance organizers and why are they an effective teaching method for teacher-centered techniques? How might Mrs. Schwarz use organizers most effectively in her instruction?

l. What visual aids does this teacher use? Why are they effective for student learning?

m. Why is summarizing student learning an important step during instruction? Where do you see evidence of this in the case? Was it effective? What other ways might teachers engage students in summarizing a lesson's main points?

n. Why do you think it is helpful for teachers to help students see connections between what they are learning and their everyday experiences? How could the teacher have used this when she is teaching science or writing?

o. Describe the importance of practice during in-class assignments. Why is it helpful for students to see worked examples as they practice important academic skills? Discuss the importance of assigning work at an appropriate difficultly level and the connection to Vygotsky's zone of proximal development.

p. Explain the role of taxonomies of educational objectives in planning.

2. Use of Technology in Instruction:

a. In today's world, technology is a daily part of children's lives. Discuss the importance of a teacher's being proficient in and using technology in the classroom.

b. Discuss the effectiveness of this teacher's use of technology in her instruction. Do you feel it is useful in helping students to learn? Why or why not?

c. What potential problems must teachers be aware of that may occur when assigning projects that require technology for students to complete at home? Speculate on some ideas that teachers could employ to assist parents who either do not have the means or the knowledge to help their students with technology.

d. The teacher in the case was not expecting to have some of the problems that she is encountering with this project. Could some of these complications have been anticipated and planned for?

e. How much control should teachers have as to the websites that students research?

f. Judge the effectiveness of a handbook that a teacher is sending home explaining the use of technology in the classroom. Is that likely to be effective on its own? Why or why not? What other ways can teachers ensure that students are aware of the potential dangers that using the internet can pose?

g. Identify what misconceptions the students in the case are demonstrating with regard to the dangers that the internet can pose? Is the
teacher's idea of creating a poster of the rules an effective one to deter
misunderstandings?

h. The teacher in this case is concerned in seeing that the use of technology-
infused instruction is not having the same benefits across all subject
areas. Outline ideas as to why this may be the case.

i. The teachers in the case bring up differences found among different
school districts budgetary considerations and the use of technology.
What tactics could schools employ to generate money or awareness of
the potential deficits in technology that some schools are faced with, as
well as the future impact on children's achievement?

3. Assessment and Instruction:

a. What relationship exists between assessment and instruction? Why is
this relationship important for teachers?

b. How is the teacher using assessment to judge the effectiveness of her
instruction?

c. Discuss how the use of technology in this case is linked to assessment
of students both formally and informally. Judge its effectiveness.

d. Do you feel that this teacher is using formative assessment effectively?

e. Discuss the benefits of teachers using both formative and summative
assessments in the classroom. How can the teacher do this in this case?

f. The teacher in the case uses technology within a project-based learning
assignment. Discuss the benefits this method has for students' learning,
as well as its disadvantages. What are tips for the effective implementation of project-based learning?

g. How can teachers incorporate alternative or performance assessments
in their classroom? What are the advantages and disadvantages?

h. Should assessments be linked to the type of material that teachers are
instructing on?

i. Discuss how online software programs for students can help teachers
track individual students' progress, as well as use informal assessment
to drive instruction.

Part VII

ASSESSMENT AND EVALUATION

Case 18

Instructional Time vs. Accountability

The Effects of State Testing

Suggested Theories: Assessment, Standardized Testing, and Controversies in Testing
Teacher Challenges: Teacher's Role in Standardized Testing, Balancing Instructional Time with State Testing, Discussing State Testing with Parents, and Student Preparation
Student Level: Upper Elementary

Camille Rogers is a new fourth-grade teacher at East Valley Elementary School. She is seated listening to the principal, Mrs. Guerrero, address the teachers about the concerns she has with regard to the poor performance that students showed on the diagnostic tests they took for the upcoming state-wide testing. "I think I can speak for all of us when I say that we are all stunned by the rather disheartening results from the practice tests. You all received your class's performance in your faculty mailboxes late last week and thus should have a copy."

Mrs. Guerrero continues, "These low test scores have serious negative implications on the school's image with the parents, the community, and the district. We have some ideas that we want to formulate into working plans, but we want to hear from you all, the teachers. I think that this can best be done in your grade groups, so I have asked every grade-team leader to meet with their teachers and address three questions: *What are the big factors influencing such poor scores? What can we do differently? How can we better prepare our students?*"

Camille watches as she fields teacher questions and many center on ESOL (English for Speakers of Other Languages) and minority students' scores. Mrs. Guerrero shares, "We are certainly aware that some minority students, as well as ESOL students, do encounter difficulties on these state tests. The ESOL students are taking a test in a language that is not their native tongue and therefore problems are expected. As educators, we are all aware that while measures have been put in place to reduce cultural biases in testing, concerns with the validity of these tests still exist as they apply to minorities and ESOL students."

She goes on to clarify that test questions are reviewed and analyzed by committees whose sole job is to monitor potential bias and ensure cultural fairness. That, in addition, questions are piloted prior to being put on the test to determine if a question presents difficulties to students from diverse backgrounds. Nevertheless, schools are required to administer the tests, and since the entire school had low scores she feels that at this time they need to focus their efforts on improving preparation and implementing strategies that could help raise test scores for all.

This meeting has taken place before school started, and now many teachers are walking back to their classrooms in clusters, using the time to further discuss some of the points of the meeting. Camille sees Lourdes Rossi and joins her on the way back to her classroom. Lourdes has been a monumental help to Camille as she settles into her teaching position, because Lourdes is a veteran teacher who also teaches fourth-grade and whose classroom is right next to hers. They immediately fall into conversation focusing on all of the lessons they are forced to revise to accommodate extra practice aimed at improving test scores.

Camille says exasperatedly, "I feel like I'm having to cut so much—it pains me to cut back on instructional activities that I know students find rewarding and challenging but that do not directly link to the state tests. Today, I upset my students when I announced I'd need to postpone two of the projects that they'd been looking forward to. One of those projects, in addition to being fun for them, would also have exposed them to authentic learning. The other one was a problem-based learning project that required collaborative, hands-on, learning which encourages higher-level processing."

"Plus," she continues, "after looking closely at the schedule, I see that we have the state testing right after the diagnostic tests. Frankly, not only am I doubting that I'll get to do the projects and activities that I have postponed, but I also don't think I'll get to incorporate many of the ideas I worked on this summer. It's frustrating because I feel like I learned so much in my teacher preparation program that I'm not sure I'll get to apply, such as instructional methods I know have great benefits for student achievement."

Lourdes nods her head in agreement and replies, "I know. You of all people know how difficult it is for me to choose to delay or completely omit activities that I feel will spark my students' creativity . . . with all the grumbling I do about how all the myriad of tests negatively impact children's imagination!" Camille agrees as the teachers part ways at the entrances to their classrooms.

Camille begins to get her classroom ready for her kids who are set to arrive shortly, and as she does so she thinks on some of the conversations she had with Lourdes and other teachers prior to the meeting. Although there seemed to be a general sense of concern over accountability, even a loss of teachers' jobs, many teachers appeared used to the stress and pressures that state testing brings, some citing that it was a definite negative of teaching while others seemed to make the best of the situation by saying they regularly use students' scores on state tests to inform their planning and teaching.

But, Camille wonders, how do they find the time to do that? Are they teaching to the test? She has heard from some teachers that they feel a tremendous amount of pressure because of the repercussions that negative test scores can have on a teacher's job and on the school in general. She definitely knew that teachers are held accountable publicly since students' scores on state tests are published.

But while limiting herself to instructing only on the skills needed for the test is bound to raise students test scores, wouldn't it also hinder their learning potential, not to mention bore the students? As a new teacher, she'd be lying if she said this wasn't keeping her up at night. Her husband just went back to school full-time to earn a master's degree and took out additional student loans to fund it; thus, she is under added financial pressure to keep her job as she is the sole income in her household.

Later that week, at the fourth-grade meeting, the teachers are all seated around a large conference table. Since East Valley Elementary is a large school, there are ten fourth-grade teachers seated around the table brainstorming ideas to communicate to the principal that center around the questions they were tasked to discuss. Bruce Durand, the fourth-grade-team leader, is responding to another teacher's comment in regard to the additional problems that state testing brings to teachers in their communications with parents.

Bruce responds, "I hear you . . . I face parents whom are mad about testing every year. Parents vary in their level of knowledge of testing, and while some parents choose to seek information with regard to state testing others really have no idea. It's difficult because some parents not only do not realize the purpose of the testing, but also do not fully understand what the test results mean or the norm-referenced nature of the scores and how the scores are used."

Lourdes interjects, "Absolutely, and then when they set up conferences to discuss these tests it can get tense—because as we all know, many parents come in and are irritated with the results blaming us for not preparing their child. And I hate to say it, but being that state testing is mandated, and that national attention is always given to education and testing, parents are going to continuously want to understand what their kids are up against—and that means coming to us." Strong agreement is heard in the room.

Camille asks the group, "If you don't mind my asking, what do you tell parents who want to help their children prepare? Because I have had parents send me e-mails and leave messages saying they're concerned with the upcoming testing." Penelope, a teacher seated next to Camille, is first to respond. "I direct them to the informational sheet I give out with study strategies and helpful hints about test preparation. I also include educational websites that have information on test preparation, advice about being prepared for the test, and sample test questions; things like children getting plenty of sleep the night before and a good breakfast."

Bruce adds, "I also send out information like Penelope says as well, but I also work with parents to help develop their children's metacognitive study skills—skills that are going to be helpful for their academic career in general. I also send home information on those strategies early on in the year with a reminder as the testing gets closer. I also identify areas in students' progress that could present problems with state testing standards and give them additional practice to do at home."

"Of course," Bruce acknowledges, "these are just suggestions and often they are not completed. When they ask me questions, I direct them to the information we have on the school website as to the goals of state testing and how educators use the results. So I try to have them see the positive side of testing, since if they have any information it is usually all the negative aspects. So for example, I let them know that state testing can determine a student's eligibility for special programs, like accelerated learning opportunities. I am also sure to remind them that we are required by law to give the test."

A few more teachers share their ideas extending on what others have said. Soon, the group is asked to break up into smaller subgroups that will later come together to determine what ideas they have brought to the table.

As Camille heads home for the day, she feels a headache starting from all the conflicting information she has learned that day with regard to state testing. While she was aware of the fact that schools were required to give them, she overlooked the emphasis that was placed on students doing well and how that impacts instruction. Some teachers are definitely using effective ways to instruct while keeping in mind state standards, but she also knows that many other teachers have shared with her that they feel the pressure to teach to the test.

She has been researching some ideas for how to help her students such as incorporating test-taking skills into all her lessons, modeling problem-solving like what is found on the test, and using some of the same vocabulary that they will encounter on the test in the lessons; however, how will she ever find the time to do this? And what if her plan on this doesn't work—what if it fails? And then she realizes she forgot to ask what she should tell the parents who have contacted her because they are considering not allowing their kids to participate in the testing.

She recalls that students who don't test are counted as not meeting the standards, and wouldn't that impact school success more so, especially with regard to funding and awards? It's no wonder teachers are so stressed, and she is also seeing it in her students. Several students have expressed endless apprehension about the upcoming state tests, and their parents seem to be preoccupied with how their results may affect their children's future. Their kids seem to be noticing, Camille feels, that they are too young to experience such strain—are they getting the pressure from home? Or is it the school atmosphere? Camille is drained and undeniably overwhelmed.

DISCUSSION QUESTIONS

1. State Testing:

   a. Discuss the goals of state testing. What are some of the advantages of testing students in this manner? What role does diagnostic testing fulfill in K–12 education?

   b. Explain how norms, validity, reliability, play a role in judging the quality of a state or standardized test.

   c. Distinguish between construct, content, and criterion validity.

   d. Compare and contrast aptitude versus achievement tests. What does each intend to measure? How are results from these tests typically used?

   e. Distinguish between a norm-referenced and criterion-referenced test. What is one obvious advantage of each type of score over the other?

2. Role of Teachers and Parents:

   a. Identify the role that a teacher plays in state testing. How are teachers held accountable for their students' performance? Include how the stress of that accountability can affect the instructional methods that a teacher uses.

   b. Discuss what test anxiety is and its application to this case. How could the teacher, Ms. Rogers, help the students who are expressing constant worry about taking upcoming state tests?

   c. Formulate ideas for what "teaching to the test" entails. Why do teachers resort to this? What negative implications does it pose for student learning and general academic success?

   d. How can teachers find a balance between covering state objectives, and standards that they will be held accountable for teaching, and student-centered forms of instruction?

e. In the case, Mrs. Rossi informs Ms. Rogers about using state testing as formative assessments. Discuss the effectiveness of this plan. Would teachers realistically have time to interpret test results to be used in this manner? How can diagnostic test results be used to guide instruction?

f. Outline what all teachers should be prepared to explain to parents in regard to state tests and how it affects their children.

g. Prepare some general tips for effective communication during parent conferences when parents come in to discuss state testing.

h. Analyze the role parents might play in helping their children prepare for standardized tests. How can teachers help parents who want to assist their children?

4. Controversies with State Testing:

a. What are the key controversies that surround state testing?

b. What are accommodations in testing that should be made for students whose native language is not English?

c. Analyze what the costs to society might be of using biased standardized tests in the schools. Can you ever free a test completely of cultural influence? If so, how? If not, why not?

d. Should performance assessments accompany standardized tests? How can authentic assessments play a role in achievement testing?

e. Evaluate the main criticisms of state-mandated testing. What are the central issues surrounding the accountability and "high-stakes testing" debate? What are the possible advantages and uses of high-stakes testing?

f. This case deals with an elementary school, however, what challenges with testing can arise at the middle and high school levels?

5. Student Preparation

a. How can teachers better prepare students for standardized testing?

b. What are some metacognitive study skills, as well as study habits, that we can teach our students?

c. What are important test-taking tips we should communicate to students? How can we help students to become expert test takers?

d. Discuss the relationship between a student's confidence in their knowledge and test anxiety.

e. In this case we see a new teacher being overcome by all of the information with regard to her role in testing. Compose your own advice about state testing that you would give to new teachers.

Index

tutoring, 83
twenty-first century learners, 93–98
twice exceptional phrase, 38

verbal conflict, 7; in early elementary,
108–9, 110; in elementary, 43; in
fifth grade, 10–13, 130–31, 132–33;
in first grade, 108–9, 110; in lower
elementary, 17, 18; in second grade,
17, 18; third grade, 43; in upper
elementary, 10–13, 130–31, 132–33
vicarious consequences, 21
vicarious punishment, 83, 123, 135
vicarious reinforcement, 83, 123, 135
video, 86–91
visual imagery, 96, 147
Vygotsky, Lev, 6, 12, 91, 147

whiteboards: ABC order, 17–18, 20;
alphabetizing, 17–18, 20; interactive,
144–45; math, 25–27
withitness: in early elementary, 7;
in elementary, 105, 122; in fifth
grade, 105, 133; in first grade,
122; in fourth grade, 83; in
kindergarten, 7; in lower
elementary, 74; in third grade,
74; in upper elementary,
83, 133
worked examples, 147
working memory, 96
writing, 147

zones of proximal development (ZPD),
6, 12, 91, 147

About the Authors

Patricia P. Willems is an associate professor of educational psychology at Florida Atlantic University, where she currently teaches both undergraduate and graduate courses in educational psychology. She earned her PhD in educational psychology from the University of Florida, and her publications are in the areas of case study instruction, learning environments, motivation, school-community partnerships, and parent involvement.

Alyssa R. Gonzalez-DeHass received her PhD in educational psychology from the University of Florida in 1998, and she is an associate professor at Florida Atlantic University. She has published in the areas of students' achievement goals, parent involvement, school-community partnerships, and the case study method to teaching educational psychology.

www.ingramcontent.com/pod-product-compliance
Lightning Source LLC
Chambersburg PA
CBHW021818270326
41932CB00007B/242